The Teacher Leader Toolkit

The Teacher Leader Toolkit

A Collection of High-Performance Strategies

Matthew J. Jennings

ROWMAN & LITTLEFIELD
Lanham • Boulder • New York • London

Published by Rowman & Littlefield
An imprint of The Rowman & Littlefield Publishing Group, Inc.
4501 Forbes Boulevard, Suite 200, Lanham, Maryland 20706
www.rowman.com

86-90 Paul Street, London EC2A 4NE, United Kingdom

Copyright © 2022 by Matthew J. Jennings

All rights reserved. No part of this book may be reproduced in any form or by any electronic or mechanical means, including information storage and retrieval systems, without written permission from the publisher, except by a reviewer who may quote passages in a review.

British Library Cataloguing in Publication Information Available

Library of Congress Cataloging-in-Publication Data
Names: Jennings, Matthew, author.
Title: The teacher leader toolkit : a collection of high-performance strategies / Matthew J. Jennings.
Description: Lanham : Rowman & Littlefield, [2022] | Summary: "This book is intended to provide teacher leaders with a repertoire of high-quality 'tools' they can immediately and effectively use to complete their job responsibilities"— Provided by publisher.
Identifiers: LCCN 2022012026 (print) | LCCN 2022012027 (ebook) | ISBN 9781475863949 (cloth) | ISBN 9781475863956 (paperback) | ISBN 9781475863963 (epub)
Subjects: LCSH: Teachers—In-service training. | Group work in education. | Mentoring in education. | Teachers—Professional relationships. | Educational leadership.
Classification: LCC LB1731 .J394 2022 (print) | LCC LB1731 (ebook) | DDC 370.71/1—dc23/eng/20220425
LC record available at https://lccn.loc.gov/2022012026
LC ebook record available at https://lccn.loc.gov/2022012027

Contents

Acknowledgments   vii

1	Introduction	1
2	Group Leadership Tools and Strategies	3
3	Leading Professional Learning Activities	17
4	Data Collection Tools for Observations	31
5	Leading Teacher Action Research	57
6	Examining Student Work	67
7	Mentor Program Coordinator Materials	71

About the Author   101

Acknowledgments

I want to thank my wife, MaryAnn Jennings, for her help with the formatting of this text. I would also like to thank my daughter, Tara Jennings, for her proofreading and revision suggestions. The time you put in helping me bring this manuscript to fruition was invaluable.

• 1 •

Introduction

*I*magine that you are a carpenter. You head out the door to the job site with your toolbox. How effectively will you complete the job you are contracted for if you bring the wrong tools? What if the tools you have are poor quality? How would those purchasing your services react if you kept choosing the wrong tools for the task and used the right tools incorrectly? At a minimum, those who hired you would doubt the potential quality of your work. People expect that a contractor hired to do a job will both have the correct tools and know how to use them.

Similarly, teachers expect teacher leaders to have an extensive "toolbox" containing strategies they can use to improve teacher effectiveness. A toolbox is an apt metaphor for this book. This book provides teacher leaders with a repertoire of high-quality "tools" they can use effectively to complete their job responsibilities.

Just as a high-quality toolbox contains the right type of tools necessary for completing the most common tasks, this book provides teacher leaders with strategies they can immediately use to handle most of their responsibilities. Of course, some of the tools in a toolbox, like a pencil and a ruler, are commonly used. Similarly, some of the strategies in this book apply to all teacher leaders, regardless of roles and responsibilities. Other tools have a very limited purpose and thus are only used for specific tasks. In the same way, some strategies presented in this book will only apply to teacher leaders with specific responsibilities. In a jam, sometimes a tool can be used to meet an unintended purpose. Similarly, with appropriate revisions, some of the strategies in this book may be adapted for other uses.

Having the right tools for the job is important. Also important is having tools that work correctly and reliably. The strategies contained within these pages have been successfully used to complete the tasks they are intended for.

Of course, you can't just pick any tool from a toolbox and hope it works. The tool must be appropriately matched to the task. For each strategy, I provide an overall description, ideas for when it should be used, and an explanation for why it should be used. This information will help you pick the correct tool for the task. Lastly, even the best tools are less effective in the hands of those who do not know how to use them. Every strategy in this book contains the required procedures for correct use. Through providing the procedures for each "tool," I am confident that each teacher leader's toolbox will be expanded to make them more effective and efficient.

Teacher leadership is a challenge. Frequently, those selected to serve as teacher leaders have no formal training and are provided with limited guidance. The tools in this toolbox will make it possible for the reader to become a "master craftsman," capable of building a better future for teachers and their students.

• 2 •

Group Leadership Tools and Strategies

High-impact teacher leaders are skilled in the use of a wide variety of collaborative tools and methods. The ability to incorporate these tools into the leadership of groups yields more efficient use of time and higher-quality products. The focus of my book *Improving Student Achievement through High-Impact Teacher Leadership* is on group process tools. More specifically, tools designed to help team members solve problems and make decisions are introduced there.

In addition to introducing several new group process tools, this chapter addresses task completion and planning tools. Task completion tools facilitate group understanding of work processes and systems. Understanding the sequence of activities and how roles and responsibilities interact makes it more likely that process improvements will target the correct actions.

Planning tools are valuable for mapping out future work. More specifically, planning tools encourage thinking that begins with the end in mind. Working backward from the end of the project, activities can be sequenced, and responsibilities can be assigned.

Lastly, this chapter concludes with activities designed to facilitate the process of team development. More specifically, four activities are provided for the introduction of group members. Additionally, an evaluation form is provided to assess the quality of group meetings.

ADDITIONAL GROUP PROCESS TOOLS

A helpful tool for making choices between items is an effort/impact grid. An effort/impact grid is a matrix that can be used to compare ideas against two criteria: the level of impact for an idea and the amount of effort required to implement it (see figure 2.1). When using this tool, it is very important for the group to discuss and agree in advance on definitions for the terms *low effort*, *high effort*, *low impact*, and *high impact*. Failure to achieve common understanding of these terms may result in very different opinions. Once this understanding is achieved, the group sorts each option as low effort with high impact, low effort with low impact, high effort with high impact, or high effort with low impact. Usually, the best options fall into the category of low effort with high impact.

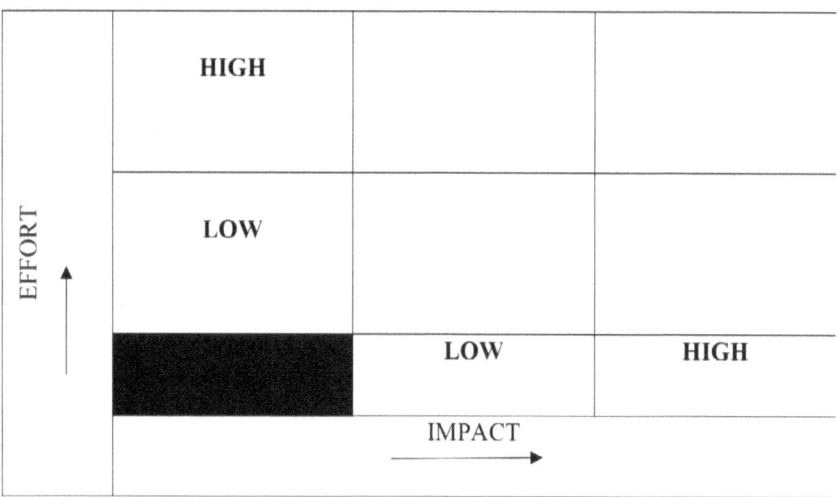

Figure 2.1

Affinity Diagram

After brainstorming, there are times when a group needs to organize and consolidate ideas. Creating an affinity diagram is an idea-generation process that can be used to accomplish this goal. Affinity diagrams are especially useful for organizing ideas generated for problem solving and then grouping ideas prior to attempting to reach agreement.

Purpose: Generating, organizing, and consolidating ideas in a group setting
Time required: 15–20 minutes
Materials:
- Sticky notes
- Chart paper

Procedure:
1. In groups of four to six individuals, brainstorm ideas by writing one idea per sticky note. When writing sticky notes, participants must:
   - Use short words or phrases.
   - Write legibly.
   - Write large enough so the item can be seen from several feet away.
2. After the allotted time, individuals post their notes randomly on a piece of chart paper.
3. Silently, individuals sort the notes into groups or categories. Anyone can move a note into any category, and notes may be moved until categories that make sense to the whole group have emerged. Notes that do not fit into a category may be placed off to the side.
4. When general agreement among group members is achieved, participants may begin talking. Discussion should result in finalizing the categories.
5. Together, participants are to write a succinct phrase that captures the theme or central idea for each category. Place this statement immediately above the cluster of ideas.

Nominal Group Technique

Sometimes a group must address controversial issues. When this happens, group activities that require high levels of interaction among members can be counterproductive. The nominal group technique is a method of brainstorming and narrowing down a list of options without the characteristic level of interaction usually found in group work.

Purpose: Generating and narrowing down a list of options for a controversial issue

Time Required: 30–45 minutes

Materials:
- Index cards
- Chart paper

Procedure:
1. In advance, define the task as a question.
2. Introduce the question to the group, and provide the opportunity to ask clarifying questions. Do not allow this to become a discussion of the issue itself.
3. Provide time for group members to silently generate solutions.
4. When the allotted amount of time is exhausted, go around the group and have each member read one idea off his or her list. Group members should cross ideas off their lists that have already been stated. Record these

ideas on a flip chart. Continue until the ideas on everyone's list have been crossed off. There cannot be any discussion at this point in the activity.

5. The group leader provides the opportunity for members to ask questions about any item listed. The person contributing the idea answers the question. Other group members may also join the discussion to help define and focus the wording.
6. The group leader facilitates the group in condensing the ideas. No member is allowed to remove an item unless the member originating the idea agrees to its removal.
7. Provide group members with between four and eight index cards.
8. Direct group members to make their selection of potential solutions from the list by writing down one item per card.
9. Have each member rank each selected item from step 8. Each person assigns the highest point value (with four index cards, it would be a value of 4) to their top choice. They continue this process until the least preferred item is labeled 1.
10. Tally the votes. The item with the highest point total is the group's selection.
11. Review and discuss the results. If members agree on the importance of the item with the highest score, then the process ends, and the group decides what to do next. If members do not agree, then the team should focus their efforts on continued discussion of the two or three highest-scoring items.

Root Cause Analysis

Oftentimes, the problem-solving process is unsuccessful because the underlying issues are not identified. Without addressing the root causes of a problem, it is highly unlikely that potential solutions will have the desired effect. Using the root cause analysis process encourages teams to dig deeper, uncovering the real reasons underlying the problem. This process is especially useful when the group has attempted solutions that have failed or the group is stuck when attempting to address a complex problem or issue.

Purpose: Analyzing a problem to identify root causes
Time required: 10–15 minutes
Materials:
- None

Procedure:
1. Develop a problem statement. For example, "Many students in our classes did not do their homework last week."

2. Begin by asking why that problem occurs. Identify a potential cause. For example, "They did not do their homework because they forgot what they needed at school."
3. Continue asking why that occurs until you have asked why enough times to get to the last layer where the group can still take action. For example, "They forgot what they needed at school because we did not require them to write it in their planners and we did not have them check their planners at the end of the school day."
4. Once the team reaches a level they have little or no control over, the process stops. At this last controllable level, it is often valuable to verify with data if it is truly the root cause.

PROCESS MAPPING

Process mapping makes work visible. As a result, teams possess as a common frame of reference for the process of task completion. Thus, process maps can improve communication and understanding. In addition to depicting how a task is currently completed, process maps can also be used to evaluate alternative ways of organizing task completion. When done collaboratively, process mapping is an activity that provides team members with the chance to contribute ideas and see those ideas represented visually.

A flowchart is usually the best tool for completing process mapping. Flowcharts commonly consist of symbols designed to represent actions. Common flowchart symbols include those in figure 2.2. There are many

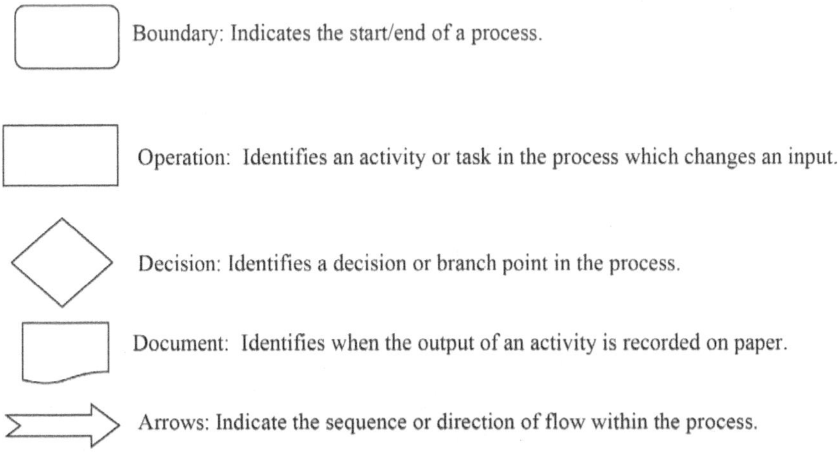

    Boundary: Indicates the start/end of a process.

    Operation: Identifies an activity or task in the process which changes an input.

    Decision: Identifies a decision or branch point in the process.

    Document: Identifies when the output of an activity is recorded on paper.

    Arrows: Indicate the sequence or direction of flow within the process.

Figure 2.2

8   Chapter 2

more possible symbols, but these are typically enough for school processes. The three types of flowcharts presented now are basic, top-down, and cross-functional.

Basic Flowchart

A basic flowchart is commonly used to generate a high-level visual of how a task is completed (see figure 2.3). Basic flowcharts are most appropriate for gaining a general overview of how a system or process operates. The following steps should be used to create a basic flowchart:

1. Decide where the process or system begins and ends.
2. Using sticky notes, brainstorm the major steps that occur between the beginning and end. Each step should consist of a verb ("review résumés") instead of topics ("résumés").
3. Sort the steps into a sequential order.

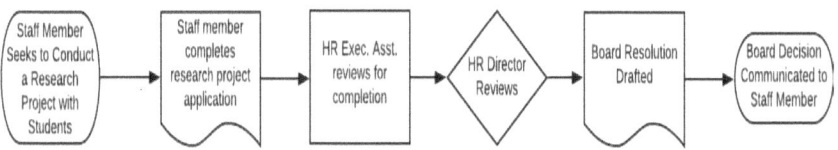

Figure 2.3

Top-Down Flowchart

A top-down flowchart depicts the major steps of the process and provides added detail vertically, below each of the major steps (see figure 2.4). This type of flowchart is used when the team wants to organize their work around major parts of a process. The following steps should be used to create a top-down flowchart:

1. Complete the steps of the basic flowchart. Number the steps (1.0, 2.0, 3.0).
2. Identify the substeps required to complete each major step.
3. List the substeps in sequence below the appropriate major step. Number these substeps (1.1, 1.2, 1.3). Numbering helps the team to communicate.

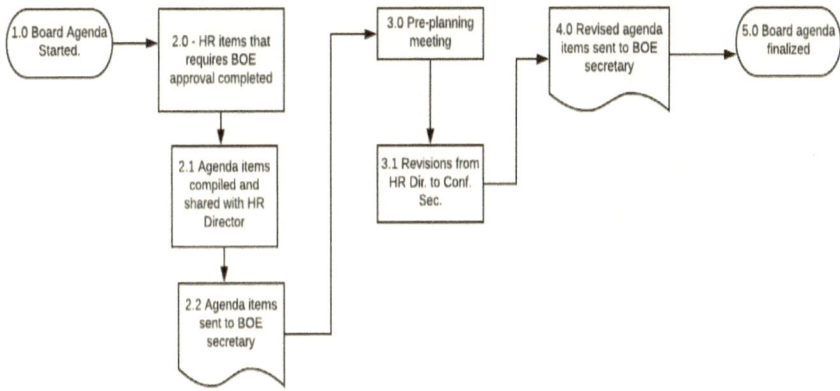

Figure 2.4

Cross-Functional Flowchart

A cross-functional flowchart is used to visually represent which individuals or groups play a role in each step of a process (see figure 2.5). It is useful for a team when they want to depict which aspects of their work are the responsibilities of specific individuals or groups. Cross-functional flowcharts are especially helpful for identifying areas of duplication, assigning tasks, and planning a new process. The following steps should be used to create a cross-functional flowchart:

1. On index cards or sticky notes, write the names of groups or individuals who work on a process. Place them across the top of a flip chart.
2. Identify the beginning and end of the process.
3. Using sticky notes, brainstorm the steps in the process.
4. Starting with the first step, place the steps in order. Move down the flowchart in order of time.
5. Place each step under the person or group who has the primary responsibility for that step. If other groups or individuals play a role in a step, then use an oval under those columns for that step. Connect the ovals to the primary step with a straight line.
6. Draw arrows connecting the primary flow of the work between the groups represented on the chart.

10   Chapter 2

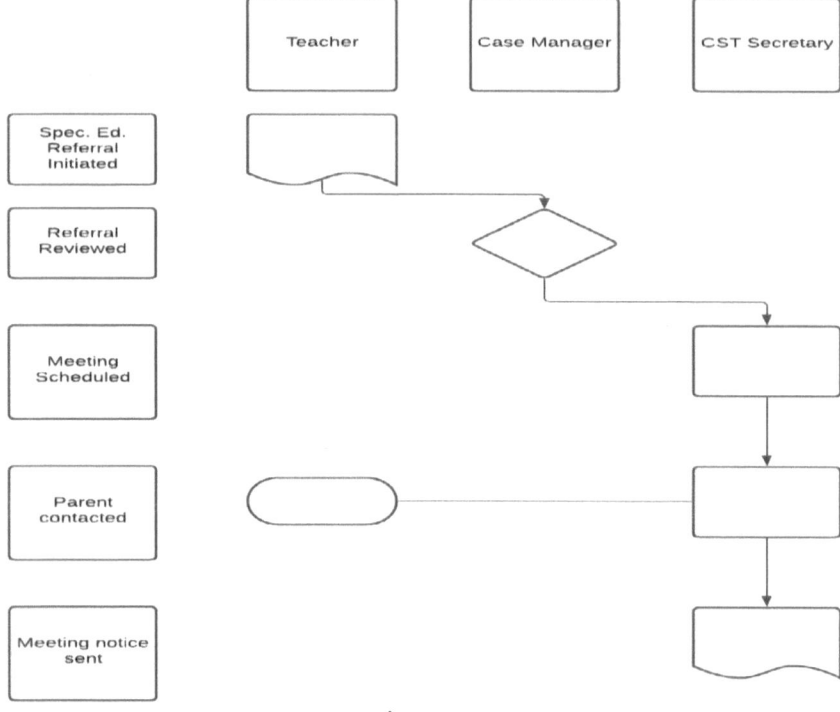

Figure 2.5

PLANNING TOOLS

Although planning adds time to implementation, it increases the chances of success and decreases wasted time. Effective groups anticipate the resources needed, potential challenges, and steps required to complete their task. In addition, these groups identify responsibilities and outcomes to be produced.

Force-Field Analysis

A force-field analysis is a productive tool for helping teams identify the barriers and supports that may affect implementation. Once a team has selected an option, a force-field analysis assists the group with identifying "driving forces" and "restraining forces." Driving forces are factors that support implementation. Restraining forces are factors that impede implementation. The goal for this activity is to identify actions that strengthen the driving forces and weaken the restraining forces. These actions become part of the implementation plan.

Purpose: Identifying factors that support and impede implementation
Time Required: 15–20 minutes
Materials:
- Flip-chart paper
- Markers

Procedure:
1. Draw two columns on a flip chart. Label one column "driving forces" and the other column "restraining forces."
2. Facilitate the team effort to brainstorm potential driving forces and then restraining forces. Write the ideas in the appropriate columns.
3. Clarify items to ensure there is common understanding of each item. Eliminate duplicates and group similar items.
4. Check the list for completeness by determining if there is a counterbalancing force for each force listed.
5. Identify actions to address key forces.

Tree Diagram

Tree diagrams assist groups with identifying essential components of a plan. They are useful when the group needs to align efforts toward a specific goal. These diagrams are especially useful for identifying the major tasks and activities required for achieving a goal (see figure 2.6).

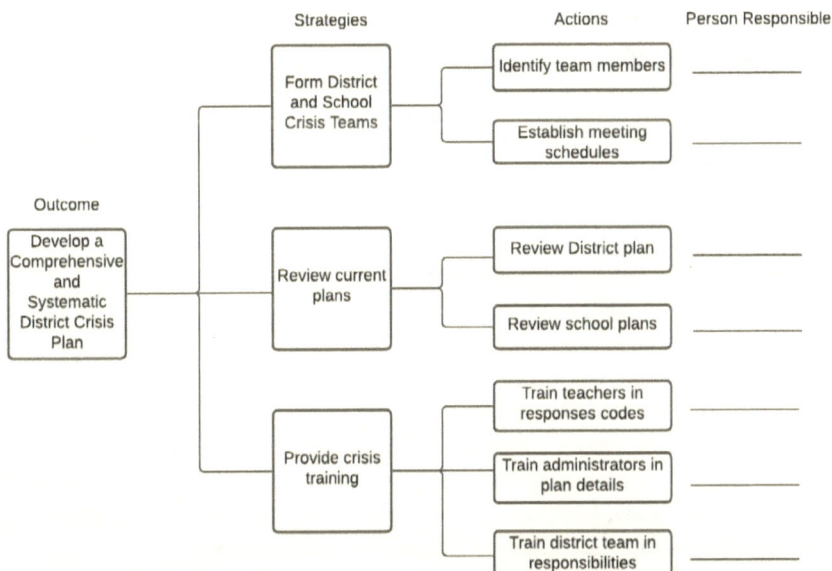

Figure 2.6

Purpose: Identification of the major steps required to complete a planning goal

Time Required: 20–30 minutes

Materials Required:
- Flip-chart paper
- Markers

Procedure:
1. Write a desired outcome at the far left in the middle of the paper. Outcomes are the desired end results of a planning process.
2. Next to the outcome, record the strategies required to accomplish the desired outcome.
3. To the right, record the specific actions that comprise each strategy.
4. To the right of each task, identify who will take responsibility for the task and when it will be accomplished.

Gantt Chart

Gantt charts are scheduling tools to capture the relative timing of process steps. These charts are useful when a group needs to determine the timing of a series of action steps. Gantt charts are especially useful after a group has identified the action steps required to complete a task (see figure 2.7).

Purpose: Scheduling the steps required for completing an action plan

Time Required: 15–20 minutes

Materials Required:
- Flip-chart paper
- Markers

Procedure:
1. Either brainstorm the actions required or list the actions already identified.
2. Sequence the action steps down the left-hand side of a grid.
3. Across the top of the grid, list the appropriate time intervals over which the plan will be implemented.
4. Estimate the length of time required to complete each action.
5. Determine the start date for each action.
6. For each action, draw a block that begins with the starting date for that step and extends through the expected duration. Color in these blocks.
7. Review the chart, identifying any potential conflicts in timing, resources required, and so on. Adjust the schedules as necessary.

ANNUAL TEACHER RECRUITING PROCESS

	October	November	December	January	February	March	April	May
Establish Recruiting Message and Themes	■							
Create Recruiting Materials		■						
Identify Projected Staffing Needs			■		Task 2			
Train Interviewers in the Interview Process								
Develop Social Media Sites Appealing to Potential Applicants					■			
Visit College Recruiting Fairs						■		
Review Recruiting Efforts and Outcomes								■

Figure 2.7

TEAM INTRODUCTIONS

Depending on how well group members already know each other, it can be appropriate to do ice-breaker activities as a means of introduction. For teams with a low degree of familiarity, these should be low-risk activities designed to begin the process of getting acquainted. As the degree of familiarity increases, so can the risk level for the activity.

The length of ice-breaker activities will also vary. For groups that will be working together for an extended period of time, a longer ice-breaking activity can be appropriate. For groups designed to last for a short duration, ice-breakers should be short. The following are ice-breaking activities a teacher leader can use to facilitate introductions.

Group Member Introductions

Purpose: Introduction of group members—especially appropriate for the first meeting of a group that has a low degree of familiarity
Time Required: 5–10 minutes
Materials:
- None

Procedure:
1. Starting with the teacher leader, group members introduce themselves. Everyone shares the following:

- Name
- Position
- A recent success in their work
- An aspect of their work they find challenging
- How they got to be a member of this group

Paired Introductions

Purpose: Introduction of group members—especially appropriate for the first meeting of a group with some familiarity

Time Required: 5–15 minutes (varies based on group size)

Materials:

- Flip-chart paper

Procedure:

1. Prior to the meeting, write the following questions on a flip chart. Post the chart in a location where it can be seen by all participants.
2. Pair up members who do not know each other well. Have them get acquainted by answering each of the following questions:
   - What is your name?
   - What is your job?
   - How long have you been with the school district?
   - What do you like best about your job?
   - What is your favorite thing to do on the weekend?
3. After each pair has answered the questions, have partners introduce one another to the rest of the group.

Flip-Chart Introductions

Purpose: Introduction of group members—especially appropriate for the first meeting of a group with a moderate degree of familiarity

Time Required: 20–30 minutes

Materials:

- Flip-chart paper
- Markers

Procedure:

1. Each member takes a turn at the flip chart (teacher leader goes first), talking about and writing down responses to one or more of the following topics:

- Tell us about your hometown. What was its name? Describe three or four of its characteristics that you find most memorable.
- Describe your first full-time job. What was the title? What parts of the job did you like and not like? What did you learn about the working world from that job?
- Draw a time line from birth to now. Divide the time line into five sections. For each section, write an important event from your life. Describe the events.

Common Denominators

Purpose: Increase participants' knowledge about group members—especially appropriate activity for groups that have a high degree of familiarity

Time Required: 10–15 minutes

Materials Required:
- None

Procedure:
1. Group members form pairs.
2. Instruct the pairs to search for traits they have in common that might make them unique from other group members. For example, both partners have traveled to Peru.
3. The answers cannot be stated negatively (i.e., traits that neither partner has). They cannot say, for example, that neither has ever traveled to Africa.
4. Have partners share their answers with the rest of the group.

MEETING EVALUATION

Meetings are processes. Thus, they can be studied and improved like any other process. Every meeting should be analyzed to identify what has worked well and what requires improvement. In addition, proactively evaluating meetings makes it possible to identify and then address issues before they become serious.

Evaluations of meeting processes do not need to be lengthy or complicated. Evaluations can take the form of round-robin sharing, in which each group member shares his or her comments in turn. Evaluations can also take the form of an open discussion. A more structured approach is a written evaluation. See table 2.1 for an example meeting evaluation form.

Table 2.1. Meeting Evaluation Form

We remained on topic.	Strongly Agree	Agree	Disagree	Strongly Disagree
The pace of the meeting was appropriate.	Strongly Agree	Agree	Disagree	Strongly Disagree
Everyone had the opportunity to participate.	Strongly Agree	Agree	Disagree	Strongly Disagree
The purpose of the meeting was clear.	Strongly Agree	Agree	Disagree	Strongly Disagree
The outcomes of the meeting were productive.	Strongly Agree	Agree	Disagree	Strongly Disagree
We followed our ground rules.	Strongly Agree	Agree	Disagree	Strongly Disagree

Regardless of the form evaluations take, if they are to be useful, then the content must be used to improve future meetings. Reflection without action will lead to frustration. If the effort is put forth to evaluate the quality of the meeting, then identified opportunities for improvement must be addressed in subsequent meetings.

• 3 •

Leading Professional Learning Activities

The content of this chapter is for teacher leaders who are responsible for providing workshops. It is often assumed that teachers' repertoires will provide them with the strategies needed to instruct adults. It is true that some of the activities used with students can be used with adults. However, adults do have unique learning needs, and the structure of workshops is not the same as a period in a classroom. This chapter provides workshop leaders with activities for opening, content processing, and closing a workshop.

OPENING A WORKSHOP

The opening segment of a training session is crucial for a successful learning experience. Participants will make up their minds, determining whether the speaker is worth listening to, in a very short period of time. A presenter does not get a second chance to make a positive impression. In the first ten minutes, a presenter must engage the participants' positive emotions, set the tone for the remainder of the training, and manage the participants' stress levels.

Engaging participants' positive emotions requires providing a safe environment. It is emotion, not logic, that drives participants' attention, meaning making, and memory. Workshop attendees must feel welcome, included, and valued.

Setting the tone for the remainder of the training requires that the presenter provides the "big picture" for participants. Thus, the presenter must provide an overview of the goals for the training and how they will be achieved.

Often, adult workshop participants come into a training session carrying outside concerns. They may be distracted and are likely concerned about the other responsibilities they could be addressing if they were not present at the training. If they are feeling high levels of stress, they will not be able to adequately focus on the content being presented. Fun, brief, easy, and interactive activities can help transition participants into the workshop and ease stress. Appropriate humor is also effective for accomplishing this goal.

Professional development providers who have a sense of humor are more likeable and effective than those who don't. Some people are naturally adept at being funny. However, a presenter doesn't need to be a naturally born comedian to bring humor into presentations. Every presenter can bring humor into their workshop by using comic strips, funny pictures or illustrations, funny quotes, and humorous videos.

Always remember that the goal is to have the group laughing together and not at the expense of any individual. Neither is it okay to get a laugh at the expense of others, nor is it alright to make racist or sexist comments. These types of statements make the presenter appear unprofessional and undermine credibility. When an audience laughs together, they bond. When that bonding occurs, the teaching and learning process become more joyful.

The following activities can be used after the introduction and workshop overview. If the group is unfamiliar with one another, then it is best to use activities that form pairs. Even strangers are usually comfortable talking to one other person. Additionally, unfamiliar groups should be given low-risk activities to complete. For groups that have a higher degree of familiarity, the presenter can start with activities designed for teams of four to six and can use activities that involve more interpersonal risk.

Activity 1: Wall Charts

Purpose: Relieve tension and provide focus on the topic
Time Required: 5–10 minutes
Materials:
- Six to eight prepared wall charts
- A prepared visual of the questions

Procedure:
1. The trainer places six to eight flip-chart sheets on the walls. Each chart should contain a quote, saying, or statistic from the training content.
2. The trainer posts a list of prompts, such as:
    - Find one statement that intrigues you.
    - Find one item that you agree with.
    - Find one thing that you might question.

3. Participants list their answers on a piece of paper and then share their choices with a partner.

Activity 2: Five Things about You

Purpose: Alleviate personal tension and help participants become acquainted
Time Required: 5–10 minutes
Materials:
- One sheet of open-ended sentence prompts per person

Procedure:
1. The presenter hands out sheet of open-ended sentence prompts (at least ten; some work-related, others personal).
2. The presenter directs participants to select and then complete five of the sentence stems.
3. Participants then share responses with a partner.

Sample Prompts:
- My three all-time favorite movies are . . .
- In high school, I was considered . . .
- Outside of work, I like to . . .
- My favorite food is . . .
- My favorite book is . . .
- The best part of being a teacher is . . .
- The worst part of being a teacher is . . .
- If I could change one thing about education, it would be . . .
- If I could have one item for my classroom, it would be . . .
- As a student teacher, I wish I had known that . . .

Activity 3: Name Tents

Purpose: Provide focus for the topic and help participants become acquainted
Time Required: 5–10 minutes
Materials:
- One name tent per person
- Fine-point markers
- Visual showing a completed name tent

Procedure:
1. The presenter distributes one blank name tent per person and ensures there are enough markers for participants to choose from.
2. The presenter directs participants to complete the name tent with the following content:

- Front side: In large print, their first and last name and a visual that will help people remember them.
- Back side: The goal(s) they have for this training.
3. Participants share completed name tents with a partner.

Activity 4: The Open Cs

Purpose: Help participants to become better acquainted and relieve personal tension

Time: 5–10 minutes

Equipment:
- A sample visual of the completed four Cs

Procedure:
1. The presenter asks participants to imagine they have won the lottery.
2. The presenter directs participants to write down what they would do with that money for each of the following:
   - The **car** they would purchase
   - The **country** they would visit
   - The **career** they would choose (other than teacher)
   - The **celebrity** they would invite to dinner
3. Participants share answers with a partner.

Activity 5: You're a Tool

Purpose: Help participants become better acquainted and relieve personal tension

Time: 5–10 minutes

Equipment:
- A ruler
- A compass
- A Swiss army knife
- A hammer

Procedure:
1. The presenter shows each tool to the participants.
2. The presenter directs participants to choose which tool is most symbolic of their personality.
3. Participants share their selection and the rationale for their choice with a partner.

PROCESSING ACTIVITIES

Adequate time and structure to process workshop content is an essential part of the learning process. Short-term memory has limited capacity. Processing activities move information out of short-term memory, thus freeing space to acquire new information. Without time to process content, participants will not be able to sort out and then store information in long-term memory. In sum, without adequate time and structure for the processing of content, a workshop is nothing more than a lecture.

A presenter must provide time for workshop participants to reflect on content and determine if or how it applies to their situations. In addition, processing opportunities must be structured. A lack of structure is likely to lead to participants doing nothing more than socializing.

Lastly, besides benefiting participants, providing processing time can benefit the trainer. The results of processing activities can serve as a gauge for the presenter to determine if workshop participants comprehend the material. With this understanding, appropriate adjustments can be made.

Activity 1: Clock Buddies

Purpose: Content processing and physical movement
Time: 5–10 minutes
Materials:
- Diagram of a clock without the hands

Procedure:
1. As setup for this activity, participants circulate throughout the room, making "appointments" with other participants. They record the name of each partner on their clocks at different hours. Encourage them to have different partners for each time. At the end of this circulation, when participants are seated again, go through each hour, making sure each person has someone else for that time. If they do not have a partner, they should raise their hand. Those who raise their hands can be partnered. If it is an odd number, it is okay to form a group of three.
2. When it is time to provide an opportunity to process content, the presenter announces the time. Participants locate their partner for that time and discuss a prompt provided by the presenter. Sample prompts include:
   - If you will remember one thing from what was just presented, it is . . .
   - Currently, I am feeling . . .
   - I can use this information in my classroom by . . .

3. This activity can be used with different partners (different times on the clock) multiple times throughout the workshop.

Activity 2: Learning Logs

Purpose: Individual processing time
Time: 5–10 minutes
Materials:
- None

Procedure:
1. The presenter announces the following topics:
   - The most important things I learned from this part of the workshop are . . .
   - This content connects with or relates to the previous content because . . .
   - I can use this information in my classroom by . . .
2. Presenter provides adequate think time. Participants write their responses.
3. Participants share their responses with a partner.

Activity 3: Takeoff-Touchdown

Purpose: Content processing and physical movement
Time: 5–10 minutes
Materials:
- None

Procedure:
1. The presenter asks a question: "What did we just learn about . . ."
2. Randomly, participants "takeoff" (stand up) to share a response. They "touchdown" (sit) when they are finished.

Activity 4: Walk and Talk

Purpose: Content processing and physical activity
Time Required: 10–15 minutes
Materials:
- None

Procedure:
1. The presenter directs participants to walk in a circular fashion, in the same direction, around the perimeter of the room.

2. As they are walking, participants find a partner. Partners share ideas.
3. After sharing an idea, partners keep moving forward to find a new partner. Again they share an idea with a new partner. The process continues until the presenter calls time.

Activity 5: An M&M for Your Thoughts

Purpose: Content processing

Time Required: 5–10 minutes

Materials:
- Enough M&Ms for each participant to have between four and six

Procedure:
1. The presenter directs participants to line up the specified number of M&Ms in a row.
2. Participants are told that they will be sharing one item (ideas, important points, etc.) for each M&M.
3. As each item is shared, the participant may eat that piece of candy.
4. The process continues until all the candy is gone.

Activity 6: Cooperative Reading

Purpose: Content processing

Time Required: 15–20 minutes, depending on the length of the article

Materials:
- One copy of a short article related to the workshop topic

Procedure:
1. Divide the staff into pairs, and provide each staff member with a photocopy of the article.
2. Each participant is directed to silently read the article.
3. One person from each pair summarizes the contents of the article, while the other partner listens carefully and provides feedback to his or her partner on the accuracy and completeness of their summary.
4. Both individuals relate the information from the article to something they already know.
5. Both partners work together to decide on and write out three or more implications for their teaching.
6. Each member of the pair finds a new partner and shares the items from their list, adding at least one new item from their new partner's list.

24 Chapter 3

Activity 7: Jigsaw

Purpose: Content processing
Time Required: 20–30 minutes, depending on the length of the reading
Materials:
- One copy of an article related to the workshop topic—can be a longer article that has parts that are not built on each other for understanding

Procedure:
1. Prior to the activity, the leader must divide the reading into three relatively equal parts.
2. Divide participants into groups of three.
3. Within each group, assign a different section of the article to each member.
4. Inform participants that the goal is for all group members to understand the content of the entire reading.
5. Ask all group members to leave their groups and pair up with someone assigned to the same section.
6. Inform participants that they have two goals: (1) to become experts in their assigned sections and (2) to plan how to teach the content of their assigned section to the members of their original group.
7. When these goals have been achieved, direct participants to return to their original groups.
8. Each member teaches his or her section of the article to the other group members.
9. When the groups have finished, randomly select a few participants to summarize the content of the entire article.

Activity 8: Problem Trade

Purpose: Content processing and problem solving
Time Required: 10–15 minutes
Materials:
- Paper
- Pencils

Procedure:
1. Share the focus prompt with participants.
2. Divide participants into groups of three to four.
3. Ask participants to discuss the focus prompt in their groups.

4. Each group writes down a problem that the group members had or anticipate having related to this topic. They must also include a solution-seeking question.
5. Going clockwise, groups trade papers.
6. Group members brainstorm potential answers to these questions, recording solutions on the papers received.
7. When time is up, each group returns the paper to the original group.
8. The original group reviews the provided solutions and decides which are feasible. Each group then reports the best idea or ideas they have received.

Activity 9: Give to Receive

Purpose: Content processing and problem solving
Time Required: 5–10 minutes
Materials Required:
- Paper
- Pencils

Procedure:
1. Direct participants to individually list ideas for addressing the problem presented.
2. After it appears most participants are finished, tell participants to stand up.
3. Direct participants to stand up and form pairs.
4. Participants take time sharing ideas.

Activity 10: Stand Up, Hand Up, Pair Up

Purpose: Content processing and movement
Time Required: 5–10 minutes
Materials Required:
- None

Procedure:
1. Direct participants to stand up, push in their chairs, and raise their hands.
2. Direct participants to take a specified number of steps in any direction.
3. Direct participants to partner with someone standing near them. Once they have formed a pair, they are to lower their hands. If there is an odd number of participants, have that individual join a pair to form a group of three.
4. Provide a discussion prompt.

5. Provide participants with a specified amount of time to discuss the prompt.
6. Once time has expired, direct participants to return to their seats.

CLOSING ACTIVITIES

Ending a training positively is as important as having a strong opening. As the presenter, you want participants to leave believing that the content was valuable and that they have ideas to implement upon their return to the classroom. It is never acceptable to simply run out of time due to poor planning.

A strong closing requires participants to form a plan of action and make connections with the content presented throughout the training. Furthermore, it is important to use celebration as a means of finishing on a high note.

Activity 1: Flip-Chart Race

Purpose: Review course content
Time Required: 10–15 minutes
Materials:
- Flip-chart paper with a vertical line down the middle of the sheet. On the left-hand side, the letters A–M are listed vertically (one letter per line). Past the midpoint of the flip chart, the letters N to Z should be listed.
- Markers

Procedure:
1. Participants are divided into teams. The size of the teams will depend on the size of the group.
2. Teams stand in a single-file line several feet from the flip chart.
3. On the presenter's signal to start, the first person goes up to the chart and writes a word or phrase from the training that starts with the letter. The letters do not need to be completed in order.
4. After recording a response, the participant runs back and hands off the marker to the next person in line. They then go to the back of the line.
5. The next participant runs up and adds a word or phrase to the chart for a different letter.
6. The process continues until the flip chart is filled, the trainer calls stop, or one round is completed.

Activity 2: Candy Bar Paragraphs

Purpose: Review course content

Time Required: 10–15 minutes

Materials:

- An assortment of miniature candy bars with names that lend themselves to the training concepts. For example, Smarties, Pay Day, 3 Musketeers, Mounds, and so on.

Procedure:

1. Each member of a small group is given a different candy bar.
2. Working together, group members are to write a paragraph that connects the name of the candy bar with what they have learned.
3. In turn, each small group shares their creation.

Activity 3: Letter to Myself

Purpose: Review content and action planning

Time Required: 5–10 minutes

Materials:

- Self-addressed, stamped envelope

Procedure:

1. Each participant is to write a letter to him- or herself. The letter is to include major points covered during the training and steps they will take after the training to implement the content in their classrooms.
2. The presenter collects the letters in each participant's sealed, self-addressed, stamped envelope.
3. The presenter mails the letters to the participants thirty days after the training.

Activity 4: Geometric Close

Purpose: Review course content

Time Required: 5–10 minutes

Materials:

- A visual containing a square, circle, right angle, and arrow

Procedure:

1. The presenter directs participants to respond to the following:
    - Think of something in the training that "squared" with what you already thought.

- Think of something in the training that made you view something from a new "angle."
- Think of something that completed or closed your "circle" of knowledge.
- Think of an action or a new approach you will take as a result of the training (arrow).
2. Have participants share their responses with a partner or in small groups.

Activity 5: Parting Messages

Purpose: Celebrating and recognizing accomplishments
Time Required: 15–20 minutes
Materials:
- Sheets of 8½" × 11" paper
- Masking tape
- Water-based markers

Procedure:
1. The presenter puts a stack of white paper and several rolls of masking tape out for participants.
2. The presenter directs participants to form pairs. Using the masking tape, each participant tapes two overlapping sheets of paper to their partner's back.
3. The presenter announces that this activity is a celebration intended to honor the work of the participants.
4. Using water-based markers (no bleed-through), participants mill around the room, writing positive, supportive statements on the backs of other participants. Participants must write small but legibly in order to conserve space.
5. After the allotted time, participants may read what has been written.

Workshops are effective for delivering content to teachers. However, even the best workshops will have minimal impact without focused, sustained follow-up activities. In addition to instructional coaching and administrative observations, two methods for promoting application of workshop content are literature study groups and demonstration lessons.

LITERATURE STUDY GROUPS

Literature study enables groups of teachers and administrators to read the same professional literature and then meet on a regularly scheduled basis to discuss key points. This type of group encourages teachers and administrators to share ideas and opinions while developing a common language and understanding.

It doesn't matter if it is a book or a series of articles, as long as the content relates to the previously delivered workshop content. The one caveat to this is that whatever is selected must lend itself to frequent discussion over time. A book that requires a complete reading prior to discussion does not work. If appropriate, allowing group members to have a voice in selecting a book will increase ownership for the activities.

Large groups make it difficult for each member to participate. Thus, the ideal size for a literature study group is between six and twelve people. If a large group is unavoidable, then subgroups can be formed.

The time and place for meetings will depend on participant preferences and what is available. Some groups will meet weekly, while others will meet once a month. Some groups will meet online. Regardless of the time, place, and meeting frequency, it is crucial to the success of these groups that times, dates, and expectations for the amount of material to be covered are explicit.

If possible, the school should provide funds for any books that must be purchased. Of course, the receipt of a book should be tied to participation in the group. Also, basic refreshments should be provided. The teacher leader could provide refreshments for the first meeting, and participants could assume shared responsibility thereafter.

Facilitation of literature study groups should be done on a rotating basis. The responsible facilitator should be expected to come to the meeting prepared with a summary of the main points and several essential questions distilled from the assigned reading. Each participant should keep a log in which they record ideas they wish to discuss and new understandings they have gained from the reading. Additionally, at the end of the discussion, several minutes should be devoted to giving teachers time to describe in their logs how the content relates to their classroom and what the implications are for future use.

DEMONSTRATION LESSON

In order for teachers to apply strategies in their classroom, they often need to see them in action. Teacher leaders can provide this opportunity via explicit demonstrations of pedagogical strategies. These demonstrations can be live lessons in classrooms or videos created by teacher leaders or other teachers. If you choose to use videos from the internet, it is important to prescreen them to ensure that they represent quality instruction.

To be effective, demonstration lessons should be connected to the workshop content previously provided. In addition, teachers must be actively and deliberately involved in the observation. Teachers should be required to take notes during the observation. To meet this purpose, teacher leaders can create and provide a checklist of pedagogical actions or student behaviors to look for.

After the lesson, teachers who participated in the demonstration lesson meet with the teacher leader. The discussion of the demonstration lesson begins with observers asking questions about what they noticed. Next, the conversation proceeds to a discussion of strategies, insights, or aha moments they had while observing. The conversation concludes with a discussion of how the strategies can be used in their classrooms.

Ideally, the teacher leader will schedule a follow-up observation of the teacher using the strategy in class. After teachers have had the opportunity to learn about a strategy, have seen it modeled, and have shared ideas for using it, they should be held accountable for making an honest effort to implement it in their own classrooms. The teacher leader can use the information from these observations to plan next steps in the professional learning process.

· 4 ·

Data Collection Tools for Observations

When observing teaching, one role required of the teacher leader is gathering data. With competent, experienced teachers, the focus for data collection will be mutually agreed upon. With low-competency or novice teachers, data collection may need to be more directive. Instead of mutual agreement, data collection may be unilaterally decided upon. Perhaps the teacher has received low performance ratings, and the teacher leader has been assigned to assist them. Perhaps it is a novice teacher who does not yet have the experience to know what the most appropriate focus would be.

This chapter contains two types of observation forms. The first type is designed to gather data based on standards of best practice in academic disciplines. The indicators identified in these forms come from documents produced by either the creators of the standards or from professional organizations for that discipline. When necessary, the forms are broken down into grade-level bands. These standards-based observation forms are particularly valuable for observing in settings outside the teacher leader's content expertise.

The second type of observation form is designed to gather data on specific aspects of instruction. At the top of the observation template is a question related to the component of instruction. In addition to an explanation, the form contains sample teacher and student behaviors that demonstrate effective use of this instructional component. Lastly, the form contains a space to record observations and then generate ideas and questions for the postconference.

Teacher Name:
Observer Name:
Date:
Time:

K–2 ELA "Look For's"

Indicator	Illustrative Student/ Teacher Behavior	Evidence Observed or Gathered			
A **majority** of ELA time is spent reading, listening to, speaking, or writing about texts.	The lesson is focused on a text or multiple texts.	1	2	3	4
The texts exhibit **exceptional craft and thought and/or provide useful information**; where appropriate, the texts are richly illustrated.	The quality of the text is high—it is well written and/or provides useful information.	1	2	3	4
Questions and tasks address the text by attending to its **structure, concepts, ideas, events and details.**	Questions and tasks repeatedly return students to the text to build understanding.	1	2	3	4
Questions and tasks require students to **use details from the text to demonstrate understanding and to support their ideas** about the text.	Questions and tasks require students to cite evidence from the text.	1	2	3	4
Questions and tasks attend to the **academic language in the text**.	Questions and tasks intentionally support students in developing facility with academic language.	1	2	3	4
Questions are **sequenced** to guide students in **delving deeper** into the text and graphics.	Questions are sequenced to support and challenge students in a deep examination of text.	1	2	3	4
Instruction and materials address foundational skills by attending to phonological awareness, concepts of print, letter recognition, phonetic patterns, and word structure.	Instruction and materials coherently address the foundational skills.	1	2	3	4

1: The teacher does not provide students this opportunity, and very few students demonstrate this behavior.
2: The teacher provides students this opportunity inconsistently, and few students demonstrate this behavior.
3: The teacher provides students this opportunity consistently, and some students demonstrate this behavior.
4: The teacher provides students this opportunity consistently, and students demonstrate this behavior.

Notes:

Teacher Name:
Observer Name:
Date:
Time:

3–12 ELA "Look For's"

Indicator	Illustrative Student/ Teacher Behavior	Evidence Observed or Gathered			
The **majority** of ELA time is spent reading, listening to, speaking, or writing about texts.	The lesson is focused on a text or multiple texts.	1	2	3	4
The texts exhibit **exceptional craft and thought and/or provide useful information**.	The quality of the text is high—it is well written and/or provides useful information.	1	2	3	4
The teacher expects **evidence** and **precision** from students and **probes students' answers** accordingly.	Students habitually provide textual evidence to support answers and responses.	1	2	3	4
The teacher creates the conditions for student conversations and plans tasks where **students are encouraged to talk about each other's thinking**.	Students use evidence to build on each other's observations or insights during discussion or collaboration.	1	2	3	4
Questions and tasks address the text by attending to its **structure, concepts, ideas, events, and details**.	Questions and tasks repeatedly return students to the text to build understanding.	1	2	3	4
Questions and tasks require students to **use details from the text to demonstrate understanding and to support their ideas** about the text.	Questions and tasks require students to cite evidence from the text.	1	2	3	4
Questions and tasks attend to the **academic language in the text**.	Questions and tasks intentionally support students in developing facility with academic language.	1	2	3	4
Questions are **sequenced** to guide students in **delving deeper** into the text and graphics.	Questions are sequenced to support and challenge students in deep examination of text.	1	2	3	4

1: The teacher does not provide students this opportunity, and very few students demonstrate this behavior.
2: The teacher provides students this opportunity inconsistently, and few students demonstrate this behavior.
3: The teacher provides students this opportunity consistently, and some students demonstrate this behavior.
4: The teacher provides students this opportunity consistently, and students demonstrate this behavior.

Notes:

Teacher Name:
Observer Name:
Date:
Time:

K–2 Science "Look For's"

Indicator	Illustrative Student Behavior	Evidence Observed or Gathered			
Asking Questions (Science) and Defining Problems (Engineering)	Ask simple descriptive questions that can be tested.	1	2	3	4
Using Models	Use and develop models that represent concrete events or design solutions.	1	2	3	4
Conducting Investigations	Plan and carry out investigations to answer questions or test solutions to problems. Conduct simple investigations based on fair tests, which provide data to support explanations or design solutions.	1	2	3	4
Analyzing Data	Collect, record, and share observations.	1	2	3	4
Using Mathematics	Recognize that math can be used to describe the natural and designed worlds.	1	2	3	4
Constructing Explanations (Science) and Designing Solutions (Engineering)	Use evidence and ideas to construct evidence-based accounts of natural phenomena and design solutions.	1	2	3	4
Arguing Evidence	Compare ideas and representations about the natural and designed worlds.	1	2	3	4
Communicating Information	Use observations and texts to communicate new information.	1	2	3	4

1: The teacher does not provide students this opportunity, and very few students demonstrate this behavior.
2: The teacher provides students this opportunity inconsistently, and few students demonstrate this behavior.
3: The teacher provides students this opportunity consistently, and some students demonstrate this behavior.
4: The teacher provides students this opportunity consistently, and students demonstrate this behavior.

Notes:

Teacher Name:
Observer Name:
Date:
Time:

3–5 Science "Look For's"

Indicator	Illustrative Student Behavior	Evidence Observed or Gathered			
Asking Questions (Science) and Defining Problems (Engineering)	Ask questions and define problems that specify qualitative relationships.	1	2	3	4
Using Models	Build and revise simple models. Use models to represent events and design solutions.	1	2	3	4
Conducting Investigations	Conduct investigations that control variables and provide evidence to support explanations or design solutions.	1	2	3	4
Analyzing Data	Use quantitative approaches to collecting data. Conduct multiple trials of qualitative observations. When feasible and possible, digital tools are employed.	1	2	3	4
Using Mathematics	Use computation and mathematics to analyze data and compare design solutions.	1	2	3	4
Constructing Explanations (Science) and Designing Solutions (Engineering)	Use evidence to construct explanations that specify variables that describe and predict phenomena and to design multiple solutions to design problems.	1	2	3	4
Arguing Evidence	Critique the scientific explanations or solutions proposed by peers, citing relevant evidence about the natural and designed worlds.	1	2	3	4
Communicating Information	Evaluate the merit and accuracy of ideas and methods.	1	2	3	4

1: The teacher does not provide students this opportunity, and very few students demonstrate this behavior.
2: The teacher provides students this opportunity inconsistently, and few students demonstrate this behavior.
3: The teacher provides students this opportunity consistently, and some students demonstrate this behavior.
4: The teacher provides students this opportunity consistently, and students demonstrate this behavior.

Notes:

Teacher Name:
Observer Name:
Date:
Time:

6–8 Science "Look For's"

Indicator	Illustrative Student Behavior	Evidence Observed or Gathered			
Asking Questions (Science) and Defining Problems (Engineering)	Ask questions and define problems that specify the relationships between variables and clarify arguments and models.	1	2	3	4
Using Models	Develop, use, and revise models to describe, test, and predict abstract phenomena and design systems.	1	2	3	4
Conducting Investigations	Conduct investigations that use multiple variables and provide evidence to support explanations or solutions.	1	2	3	4
Analyzing Data	Distinguish between correlation and causation. Use basic statistical techniques of data and error analysis.	1	2	3	4
Using Mathematics	Identify patterns in large data sets and use mathematical concepts to support explanations and arguments.	1	2	3	4
Constructing Explanations (Science) and Designing Solutions (Engineering)	Construct explanations and design solutions that are supported by multiple sources of evidence and are consistent with scientific ideas, principles, and theories.	1	2	3	4
Arguing Evidence	Construct a convincing argument that supports or refutes claims for either explanations or solutions about the natural and designed world.	1	2	3	4
Communicating Information	Evaluate the merit and validity of ideas and methods.	1	2	3	4

1: The teacher does not provide students this opportunity, and very few students demonstrate this behavior.
2: The teacher provides students this opportunity inconsistently, and few students demonstrate this behavior.
3: The teacher provides students this opportunity consistently, and some students demonstrate this behavior.
4: The teacher provides students this opportunity consistently, and students demonstrate this behavior.

Notes:

Teacher Name:
Observer Name:
Date:
Time:

K–12 Mathematics "Look For's"

Indicator	Illustrative Student Behavior	Evidence Observed or Gathered			
The teacher uses strategies to keep all students **persevering with challenging problems**.	Even after reaching a point of frustration, **students persist** in efforts to solve challenging problems.	1	2	3	4
The teacher establishes a classroom culture in which **students explain their thinking**.	**Students elaborate** with a second sentence (spontaneously or prompted by the teacher or another student) to explain their thinking and connect it to their first sentence.	1	2	3	4
The teacher orchestrates conversations in which **students talk about each other's thinking**.	**Students talk about and ask questions** regarding each other's thinking in order to clarify or improve their own mathematical understanding.	1	2	3	4
The teacher connects students' informal language to **precise mathematical language** appropriate to their grade.	**Students use precise mathematical language** in their explanations and discussions.	1	2	3	4
The teacher has established a classroom culture in which **students choose and use appropriate tools** when solving a problem.	**Students use appropriate tools strategically** when solving a problem.	1	2	3	4
The teacher asks **students to explain and justify work** and provides feedback that helps students revise their initial work.	**Student work includes revisions**, especially revised explanations and justifications	1	2	3	4

1: The teacher does not provide students this opportunity, and very few students demonstrate this behavior.
2: The teacher provides students this opportunity inconsistently, and few students demonstrate this behavior.
3: The teacher provides students this opportunity consistently, and some students demonstrate this behavior.
4: The teacher provides students this opportunity consistently, and students demonstrate this behavior.

Notes:

Teacher Name:
Observer Name:
Date:
Time:

K–12 Social Studies "Look For's"

Indicator	Illustrative Student Behavior	Evidence Observed or Gathered			
Meaningful Content	Key concepts and themes are emphasized and are **developed in depth**. Skill development is embedded throughout the lesson.	1	2	3	4
Value Based	Students engage in experiences that develop fair-mindedness and encourage recognition and serious consideration for **opposing points of view, respect for well-supported positions, sensitivity to cultural differences**, and a **commitment to individual and social responsibility**.	1	2	3	4
Challenging	Instruction makes use of **regular writing** and the **analysis of various types of documents**. Students are engaged in **substantive conversations** and **disciplined inquiry**.	1	2	3	4
Active	Students work **independently and collaboratively** to reach understandings, make decisions, discuss issues, and solve problems.	1	2	3	4
Integrative	As appropriate, instruction **draws on ideas from the various social studies disciplines** to increase understanding of the event or concept.	1	2	3	4

1: The teacher does not provide students this opportunity, and very few students demonstrate this behavior.
2: The teacher provides students this opportunity inconsistently, and few students demonstrate this behavior.
3: The teacher provides students this opportunity consistently, and some students demonstrate this behavior.
4: The teacher provides students this opportunity consistently, and students demonstrate this behavior.

Notes:

Teacher Name:
Observer Name:
Date:
Time:

K–12 Physical Education "Look For's"

Indicator	Illustrative Student/ Teacher Behavior	Evidence Observed or Gathered			
The class has an effective structure.	Physical education class begins with an instant activity, anticipatory set, and physical warm-up; proceeds to the instructional focus and fitness activities; and closes with a physiological cool-down and a review of instructional objectives.	1	2	3	4
The teacher organizes his or her class to maximize opportunities for all students to learn and be physically active.	Sufficient equipment is provided so that students spend virtually no time waiting for turns or standing in lines. At least half of class time is spent in moderate to vigorous activity.	1	2	3	4
The environment is supportive of all students and promotes developing a positive self-concept.	Students are allowed to try, to fail, and to try again, free of criticism or harassment from the teacher or other students.	1	2	3	4
The teacher ensures students' safety by monitoring class closely.	The teacher remains aware of student behavior and closely supervises physical activities.	1	2	3	4
The teacher forms pairs, groups, and teams in ways that preserve every child's dignity and self-respect.	Groups are formed randomly, by fitness or skill level when necessary, or by a class system, such as birthdays, squads, colors, or numbers.	1	2	3	4
The teacher shows enthusiasm for an active, healthy lifestyle.	The teacher is positive and enthusiastic about physical education activities.	1	2	3	4

1: The teacher does not provide students this opportunity, and very few students demonstrate this behavior.
2: The teacher provides students this opportunity inconsistently, and few students demonstrate this behavior.
3: The teacher provides students this opportunity consistently, and some students demonstrate this behavior.
4: The teacher provides students this opportunity consistently, and students demonstrate this behavior.

Notes:

Teacher Name:
Observer Name:
Date:
Time:

K–12 Health Education "Look For's"

Indicator	Illustrative Student/ Teacher Behavior	Evidence Observed or Gathered			
The teacher develops and maintains a positive learning environment in which all students feel emotionally, socially, and physically safe.	The teacher develops an avenue for students to ask sensitive questions. Students collaborate, cooperate, and show acceptance of one another.	1	2	3	4
The teacher implements activities and uses materials that are current and relevant to students.	Materials are current and factually accurate. Content of materials is relevant to students' lives and/ or important for students' health. Materials are developmentally appropriate and culturally inclusive.	1	2	3	4
The teacher uses different modes of delivery and a variety of approaches to engage all students and meet the needs of all learners.	The teacher uses a balanced approach to teaching, not overly relying on one teaching strategy.	1	2	3	4
The teacher demonstrates passion and enthusiasm for health education.	The teacher is actively engaged in the instructional process. Teacher behaviors indicate enthusiasm for content.	1	2	3	4
The teacher employs instructional strategies that promote student self-reflection and help students personalize the lesson.	The teacher provides opportunities for students to reflect and apply learning to their own lives. The teacher recognizes and uses teachable moments that occur both inside and outside the classroom.	1	2	3	4
Instruction includes multiple opportunities for and emphasizes application of health-related skills.	Students are required to practice skills inside and outside the classroom. Students receive feedback on their practice attempts.	1	2	3	4

1: The teacher does not provide students this opportunity, and very few students demonstrate this behavior.
2: The teacher provides students this opportunity inconsistently, and few students demonstrate this behavior.
3: The teacher provides students this opportunity consistently, and some students demonstrate this behavior.
4: The teacher provides students this opportunity consistently, and students demonstrate this behavior.

Notes:

Teacher Name:
Observer Name:
Date:
Time:

Instructional Element: Learning Objective(s)

What does the teacher do to provide clear learning objective(s)?
The teacher clearly identifies the essential content to be learned, including the level of cognition to be attained by the student, congruent and observable proving behavior, and the expected level of performance. In addition, he or she clearly communicates the objective for the lesson to the students.

Teacher Evidence	Student Evidence
• The objective for the lesson is written so that it includes the required elements. • The differences in the essential content far outweigh the similarities. • The level of complexity is raised more frequently than the level of difficulty. • The objective is visible for students to view.	• When asked, students can clearly articulate the essential content that is the subject of the lesson. • When asked, students can clearly explain how their current activities relate to the learning objective. • When asked, students can explain how they will know they have reached the objective.
Observation Notes	**Ideas and Questions**

Teacher Name:
Observer Name:
Date:
Time:

Instructional Element: Anticipatory Set

What does the teacher do to help students focus on the most important content and connect that content to what they already know?
The teacher uses an anticipatory set to focus the students' attention on the content to be learned and to activate relevant prior knowledge. In addition, he or she uses the information provided by students to determine what students already know or can do and then adjusts if necessary.

Teacher Evidence	Student Evidence
• The teacher uses activities to determine what students already know about the topic. • When necessary, the teacher reteaches information or skills he or she thought the students had already acquired. • Teacher activities focus students' attention on the most important content to be learned.	• When asked, students can explain linkages with prior knowledge. • Students actively engage in previewing activities.
Observation Notes	**Ideas and Questions**

Teacher Name:
Observer Name:
Date:
Time:

Instructional Element: Purpose

How does the teacher help students see the purpose in the content?	
The teacher uses effective strategies to help students see the reason for learning the content.	
Teacher Evidence	**Student Evidence**
• After identifying the learning objective, the teacher explains why learning this content is important. • The teacher's explanation would likely be meaningful to the majority of the students. • The teacher cues the importance of the content through his or her tone of voice and nonverbal behaviors.	• When asked, students can describe why learning this content is important. • After hearing the explanation, students visibly adjust their level of engagement.
Observation Notes	**Ideas and Questions**

Teacher Name:
Observer Name:
Date:
Time:

Instructional Element: Input

How does the teacher provide the input students need to meet the learning objective?
The teacher effectively uses a variety of strategies to provide the information necessary for students to achieve the objective. In addition, he or she presents new information verbally and visually, uses an appropriate organizational structure for the content, chunks the content into digestible bits of information, and identifies any unique and unvarying elements that make it different from other content.

Teacher Evidence	Student Evidence
• The teacher provides the input students require for performing the skill or demonstrating the knowledge in the content of the learning objective. • The teacher clearly articulates what makes the content different from all other similar concepts. • The teacher uses a sensible, basic organizational pattern to present the information. • The teacher presents the information both visually and verbally.	• When asked, students can state the information necessary for performing the skill or demonstrating the knowledge. • When asked, students can describe how the concept is unique. • Students' notes include words, pictures, and summary statements that come from a process of revision and review.
Observation Notes	**Ideas and Questions**

Teacher Name:
Observer Name:
Date:
Time:

Instructional Element: Models and Examples

How does the teacher use models and examples to increase student understanding?	
The teacher uses models and examples to accurately and clearly highlight the crucial attributes of new content. In addition, he or she avoids controversial issues and nonexamples when first introducing the new content.	
Teacher Evidence	**Student Evidence**
<ul><li>The teacher provides models and/or examples when the learner does not have the experience to visualize the concept or generalization being taught.</li><li>The model or examples are accurate and clearly identify the crucial attributes of the new learning.</li><li>The teacher avoids controversial issues and nonexamples when first introducing the concept.</li><li>If appropriate, worked examples are provided.</li></ul>	<ul><li>When asked, students can provide an accurate model or example of the new learning.</li></ul>
Observation Notes	**Ideas and Questions**

Chapter 4

Teacher Name:
Observer Name:
Date:
Time:

Instructional Element: Checking for Understanding

How does the teacher check students' understanding?	
The teacher effectively uses a variety of methods to verify students' understanding of the content presented. In addition, he or she accurately uses this information to determine if additional input, models, or examples are necessary for increasing student understanding.	
Teacher Evidence	**Student Evidence**
<ul><li>When asking questions, the teacher provides students with a minimum of three seconds of think time.</li><li>When selecting students to provide an answer to a question, the teacher predominantly uses random selection techniques.</li><li>When a student provides the correct answer, the teacher provides an additional one to two seconds of student think time.</li><li>The teacher persists with students who do not get the correct answer.</li><li>The teacher uses whole-group participation strategies to increase the active involvement of all students.</li></ul>	<ul><li>All students are required to process an answer to questions asked.</li><li>Students silently wait for someone to be randomly selected to answer the question.</li><li>Selected students attempt to provide an answer to the question asked.</li></ul>
Observation Notes	**Ideas and Questions**

Teacher Name:
Observer Name:
Date:
Time:

Instructional Element: Guided Practice

How does the teacher structure guided practice opportunities for students?	
Depending on where the learner is in the process, the teacher provides either massed or distributed practice. This practice is short, frequent, focused, and accompanied by prompt and specific feedback.	
Teacher Evidence	**Student Evidence**
<ul><li>The teacher uses different types of practice depending on where the learners are in the process of acquiring the content.</li><li>Observed practice periods are short, frequent, and focused.</li><li>The teacher provides prompt, specific, corrective feedback to students on whether their practice is correct or incorrect and why.</li><li>Evidence of distributed practice for crucial knowledge and skills is available.</li></ul>	<ul><li>Observed student practice is correct.</li><li>Students are engaged and focused in completing practice activities.</li><li>Students voluntarily ask clarification questions and seek help as needed.</li><li>When asked, students can identify the reasons for completing the provided practice activities.</li></ul>
Observation Notes	**Ideas and Questions**

Chapter 4

Teacher Name:
Observer Name:
Date:
Time:

Instructional Element: Closure

How does the teacher provide students with an opportunity for closure?
During prime-time 2, the teacher provides students with the opportunity to summarize for themselves their perception of what has been learned. In addition, the teacher provides specific directions for what the learner should process, adequate time to accomplish this processing, and a clear description of the overt product that is required.

Teacher Evidence	Student Evidence
• The teacher provides specific directions for what the learner should process. • The teacher provides a clear description of the overt product that must be produced. • The time provided for the closure activity is sufficient.	• Students actively engage in the covert process of mentally rehearsing and summarizing the information presented. • Students' overt products indicate clear understanding of the content and task.
Observation Notes	**Ideas and Questions**

Teacher Name:
Observer Name:
Date:
Time:

Instructional Element: Independent Practice

How does the teacher provide opportunities for independent practice?
The teacher provides the learner(s) with independent practice activities that have a clear purpose. In addition, the teacher provides timely feedback on the independent practice activities completed.

Teacher Evidence	Student Evidence
• The teacher communicates a clear purpose for the independent practice activities. • The teacher provides timely feedback to students on the results of their independent practice activities.	• Students are able to complete the independent practice activities with minimal adult involvement. • When asked, students can state the purpose for completing the independent practice activities. • The students' completed work shows a high level of accuracy.
Observation Notes	**Ideas and Questions**

Chapter 4

Teacher Name:
Observer Name:
Date:
Time:

Instructional Element: Presentation Skills

How effectively does the teacher present new information?	
The teacher uses effective pacing and demonstrates enthusiasm for the content being presented.	
Teacher Evidence	**Student Evidence**
• The teacher employs "crisp" transitions from one activity to another. • The teacher alters pace appropriately. • The teacher describes personal experiences that relate to the content. • The teacher signals excitement for content with physical gestures, voice tone, or dramatization of information.	• Students quickly adapt to transitions and reengage when an activity begins. • When asked about the pace of the class, students describe it as neither too fast nor too slow. • When asked, students say that the teacher "likes the content" and "likes teaching."
Observation Notes	**Ideas and Questions**

Teacher Name:
Observer Name:
Date:
Time:

Instructional Element: Teacher-Student Relationships

How does the teacher build and maintain positive relationships with students?	
The teacher uses verbal and nonverbal behaviors to develop and maintain positive relationships with students.	
Teacher Evidence	**Student Evidence**
• The teacher compliments students regarding academic and personal accomplishments. • The teacher engages in informal conversations with students that are not academic (at the appropriate time). • The teacher uses appropriate humor with students. • The teacher smiles or nods at students. • Over time, the teacher uses the above behaviors equitably.	• When asked, students describe the teacher as someone who cares about them. • Students respond to the teacher's verbal or nonverbal interactions. • When asked, students say the teacher expects everyone to participate in class.
Observation Notes	**Ideas and Questions**

Teacher Name:
Observer Name:
Date:
Time:

Instructional Element: Rules and Procedures

How does the teacher establish classroom rules and procedures?	
The teacher develops rules and routines to encourage positive student behavior.	
Teacher Evidence	**Student Evidence**
• Rules are visible for students. • Rules are stated positively and behaviorally. • Rules are doable and manageable. • Procedures are developed for common classroom activities.	• When asked, students can state the classroom rules. • Students are able to independently follow classroom routines
Observation Notes	**Ideas and Questions**

Teacher Name:
Observer Name:
Date:
Time:

Instructional Element: Reinforcing Effort

How does the teacher reinforce effort with students?	
The teacher uses explicit strategies to foster the understanding between effort and achievement and acknowledges students' efforts when they work hard to achieve.	
Teacher Evidence	**Student Evidence**
• The teacher uses stories to establish the relationship between effort and achievement. • The teacher provides students with explicit information detailing the actions and behaviors associated with effort in various academic situations. • The teacher requires students to self-assess their effort and then record it next to their achievement results. • The teacher uses language that emphasizes effort over natural ability.	• When asked, students state that effort is necessary for and frequently leads to achievement. • Students persist when confronted with difficult academic tasks.
Observation Notes	**Ideas and Questions**

Teacher Name:
Observer Name:
Date:
Time:

Instructional Element: Physical Layout of Classroom

How does the teacher organize the physical layout of the classroom?	
The teacher organizes the physical layout of the classroom to facilitate movement and focus on learning.	
Teacher Evidence	**Student Evidence**
• The physical layout of the classroom has clear traffic patterns. • The physical layout of the classroom provides easy access to materials and centers. • The classroom is decorated in a way that enhances student learning: —Bulletin boards relate to relevant content. —Students' work is displayed.	• Students move easily about the classroom. • Students make use of classroom materials and learning centers. • Students can easily focus on instruction.
Observation Notes	**Ideas And Questions**

Teacher Name:
Observer Name:
Date:
Time:

Instructional Element: Mental Set

How does the teacher demonstrate awareness and emotional objectivity?
The teacher demonstrates awareness of the actions of all students in the classroom and behaves in a way that is objective and controlled.

Teacher Evidence	Student Evidence
• The teacher does not exhibit extremes in positive or negative emotions. • The teacher addresses inflammatory issues and events in a calm and controlled manner. • The teacher does not demonstrate personal offense at student misbehavior. • Over the course of a class period, the teacher physically occupies all quadrants of the classroom. • The teacher scans the entire classroom, making eye contact with all students. • The teacher recognizes potential sources of disruption and deals with them immediately.	• When asked, students describe the teacher as "someone who has eyes in the back of their head." • When asked, students describe the teacher as in control of the class. • When asked, students say the teacher does not hold grudges or take things personally.
Observation Notes	**Ideas and Questions**

Teacher Name:
Observer Name:
Date:
Time:

Instructional Element: Disciplinary Interventions

How does the teacher respond to student misbehavior?	
The teacher acknowledges and reinforces positive student behavior while providing appropriate negative consequences for negative student behavior.	
Teacher Evidence	**Student Evidence**
• The teacher provides **nonverbal** signals when students' behavior is or is not appropriate. • The teacher provides **verbal** signals when students' behavior is or is not appropriate. • The teacher uses direct-cost consequences when appropriate. • Occasionally, the teacher uses tangible recognition when a rule or procedure has been followed. • The teacher uses intervention strategies that are at the lowest level of "intrusiveness."	• When asked, students describe the teacher as appreciative of their positive behavior. • Students cease inappropriate behavior when the teacher uses verbal or nonverbal cues. • Students accept consequences as part of the way class is conducted. • When asked, students describe the teacher as fair in application of rules.
Observation Notes	**Ideas and Questions**

· 5 ·

Leading Teacher Action Research

Teacher action research is the planned methodical study of one's own teaching. The overarching goal of teacher action research is the collection of valid information that can be used to make informed rather than intuitive decisions. There are many models of implementation of teacher action research, but most include the following steps.

First, the teacher identifies an area of concern or interest. After doing a review of relevant existing literature, the teacher develops a problem statement and at least one research question. To answer the research question, the teacher creates an action plan and methods for data collection. After implementing the appropriate strategies and collecting the data, the teacher conducts an analysis and draws conclusions. These conclusions and their corresponding implications for practice are then shared with colleagues. Even though the steps have been listed sequentially, the process is frequently recursive. There is often repetition or alteration of steps based on how the study is progressing. In addition, the lengths of studies vary based on the nature of the problem identified. It is not a one-size-fits-all approach.

Teacher action research has multiple benefits. First, teacher action research has been proven to increase teacher knowledge directly related to classroom practice. Second, it promotes the reflective thinking required to reach an increased level of mastery. Done effectively, teacher action research results in the understanding that good teachers are good students. They are lifelong learners seeking to improve their knowledge and practice throughout their careers. Third, teacher action research addresses motivational concerns. It is a professional growth activity that fosters ownership of effective practice as well as an openness to new ideas. Fourth, by its nature, teacher action research promotes collegiality focused on substantive issues. Lastly, teacher action research promotes professionalism through the expectation that teachers will interact with and contribute to the development of the professional knowledge base. They are no longer expected to simply serve as consumers of other people's research.

Of course, as with virtually all professional growth activities, administrative leadership and support is vital to the success of teacher action research. Providing time for problem solving and collaboration is essential. If teachers at a grade level or within a department are conducting a collaborative action research project, they will require more meeting time than a project being completed individually. Yet even an individually conducted project benefits from time for the teacher to brainstorm and talk with colleagues. Part of the power of the action research process is the reflective dialogue it requires.

Teacher leaders must provide a forum for sharing the results from these studies. Sharing results of locally conducted studies is highly relevant to other staff members. The fact that these studies are done in the context of the local school or district increases the chances that other faculty members are experiencing similar issues. Therefore, findings in one teacher's classroom may have a positive impact on other teachers' classrooms. Furthermore, as a result of learning about a colleague's research, faculty members may acquire new ideas for further research of their own.

Sharing results can take many forms. The teacher leader could publish and distribute a school "academic journal" comprised of completed studies. On professional development days, projects could be shared through poster sessions. At faculty meetings, staff can share their research and findings via PowerPoint presentations. Providing forums for sharing signifies the value of both the research and the researcher.

Teacher leaders facilitating teacher implementation of action research projects must provide the basic knowledge and skills required to successfully complete the process. In addition, they must provide clear expectations regarding project parameters, deadlines, and final products. The next section of this chapter details the basic competencies required to implement a project. Also provided is a sample completed proposal and project report as well as blank copies for teacher use. Templates must be adjusted to meet local requirements and resources. All this information can be copied, distributed, and then reviewed with the appropriate faculty members near the start of implementing teacher action research.

TEACHER ACTION RESEARCH HANDBOOK

What Is Teacher Action Research?

a. Teacher action research is **planned, methodical** observation related to **one's own teaching**.

What Are the Benefits of Conducting Teacher Action Research?

a. Teacher action research assists teachers in developing new knowledge directly related to their own classrooms.
b. Teach action research encourages informed rather than intuitive decision making about classroom practices.
c. Teacher action research empowers teachers to make decisions regarding areas of interest and need.
d. Teacher action research encourages collegial dialogue focused on substantive issues of teaching and learning.

What Are the Steps for Conducting Teacher Action Research?

a. Step 1: Identify an area of interest or concern.
   - Teacher action research begins with asking, What elements of practice or what aspects of student learning do I wish to examine in depth?
   - Regardless of the area of interest selected, it must concern the teaching/learning process and be within the teacher's scope of influence.
b. Step 2: Review relevant literature.
   - Explore a range of books, articles, and reports related to your topic. Doing so will increase your knowledge of what is already known about the topic. In addition, reading relevant literature on your chosen topic may also give you ideas for new instructional strategies.
c. Step 3: Develop a problem statement.
   - Having conducted a thorough review of the literature in your area of interest, the next step is the development of a problem statement. Establishing a clear idea of what you are studying and why you are studying it is a crucial step toward successful completion of any action research project. Composing a clear and concise problem statement of approximately one hundred words focuses the remainder of the work. Your problem statement contains answers to the following questions:

1. Who is affected?
2. Who or what is suspected of causing the problem?
3. What kind of problem is it (resources, skills, time, materials, etc.)?
4. What is the goal for improvement?
5. What do you propose to do about it?
- **Example problem statement:** My students are not correctly editing the final drafts of their written work (*answers questions 1 and 3*). I believe this is because they are not using effective editing strategies (*answers question 2*). I want all students to provide final drafts that are free of grade-level grammar and spelling errors (*answers question 4*). Therefore, I will train my students and then require them to use an editing checklist (*answers question 5*).

d. Step 4: Develop a research question.
- Even though no perfect formula exists for framing an action research question, many teachers find it helpful to use the following framework: "What is the impact of _____ on _____?" In the first blank, the practice is described. The second blank names the desired impact. A research question that could be used for the earlier problem statement is "What is the impact of editing checklists on the quantity of grammar and spelling errors in final drafts?"
- Regardless of the format used, quality teacher action research questions are appropriately narrow, require higher-level thinking (not yes or no answers), are precise, avoid ambiguous terms, and can be answered by the researcher within any time constraints established. A question should be revised until it meets these criteria.

e. Step 5: Collect data.
- Before implementing any instructional interventions, the action researcher must decide the type of data required to answer their research question. They must also determine how they will systematically collect that data as well as the time frame they will follow for data collection. There are many types of data that an action researcher can collect. Types of data can be categorized as either:

    1. quantitative: data that can be measured by numbers, or
    2. qualitative: data that can be measured by descriptions.

    The choice of the type of data collected will depend on the research question. To increase the validity and reliability of findings, action researchers strive to triangulate their data. Triangulation involves collecting multiple sources of data for every phenomenon or issue being studied. Triangulation of data compensates for the imperfections of single data-gathering instruments, thus increasing confidence in results. Triangulation can be achieved by collecting the same type of data over time or by collecting different types of data on the same phenomenon of interest.

f. Step 6: Plan implementation.
- Reviewing the literature will likely have provided you with ideas for new techniques and strategies that you think will produce better results. At this stage in the process, it is important to list both the steps and time line for implementing the identified intervention(s). Taking this action will make your intervention capable of being repeated by others and will keep you focused on the appropriate implementation procedures.

g. Step 7: Analyze data.
- Once the data has been collected, it must be organized. If the data is quantitative, then tables and graphs can be used to create a visual display. If the data is qualitative, a matrix can be created to organize the data by categories.
- As you "interrogate" the data, you are looking for the patterns or themes that emerge. Once you identify these patterns or themes, the next step is to categorize the data from your study that supports each one. You are now ready to draw tentative conclusions.

h. Step 8: Report results.
- When reporting results, your audience is your fellow educators. The goals of sharing what you have learned are to share your tentative conclusions and the implications those conclusions have for classroom practice. It is absolutely acceptable for your conclusions to be different from what you had expected. Sometimes we learn just as much from what did not work as what did. In fact, this often leads to additional questions for further research. Articulating potential questions for future research is the final step in reporting the results of a teacher action research project.

As described up to this point, teacher action research appears to be a linear process. Often it is not sequential. Instead, it is frequently recursive, with revisions, adjustments, and revisiting previous steps occurring throughout the study. This fluidity is the nature of the action research process.

Chapter 5

SAMPLE TEACHER ACTION RESEARCH PROJECT

Staff Member's Name: Jane Doe	School Year: 2020–2021
I will be working to implement this plan: ___X___ Individually _____ In a Group. If in a group, please list group members:	
Problem Identification	
Interest Area: Fluency with single-digit multiplication facts	
Literature Reviewed: Lang-Raad, N. D., & Marzano, R. J. (2019). *The New Art and Science of Teaching Mathematics*. Solution Tree Press. Sousa, D. A. (2014). *How the Brain Learns Mathematics*. Corwin Press.	
Problem Statement: My students are not demonstrating fluency with single-digit multiplication. I believe this is because they are not participating in short, focused, and regular distributed practice sessions. I want all students to develop automaticity with multiplication facts. Therefore, I will implement a "Mad Minute" for multiplication as a daily warm-up for math class.	
Research Question: What is the impact of daily, one-minute multiplication practice on automaticity with single-digit multiplication facts?	
Data Collection Methods	
Data Source 1 (What and How): Preassessment of single-digit multiplication administered prior to implementation of one-minute multiplication practice sessions.	
Data Source 2 (What and How): Students will graph daily how many facts they got correct.	
Data Source 3 (What and How): Postassessment of single-digit multiplication administered upon conclusion of implementation of one-minute multiplication practice sessions.	
Implementation Schedule	
Tasks	Time Line
Administer preassessment.	November 1, 2020
Implement daily one-minute multiplication practice sessions at the beginning of each math class. Teach students to record results.	November 2, 2020
Administer postassessment.	December 23, 2020

TEACHER ACTION RESEARCH REPORT

Data Analysis
Provide a narrative summary of your collected and analyzed data. If appropriate, please attach graphs and tables to this summary.
After administering the pretest, I compiled the range, mean, and median for the class. The class average for the number of correct facts completed in sixty seconds was twenty-three. However, the range was from three to forty-six. Thus, the median of thirty-one correct facts was a more accurate reflection of class performance. During the intervention, students recorded and graphed daily results. These results were reviewed weekly. Analysis of these weekly graphs revealed that 78 percent of the students demonstrated an increased number of facts correct every week. Of this 78 percent, the majority (61 percent) demonstrated an increase of three or more correct facts weekly. Of the 22 percent of the students who did not demonstrate a weekly increase of facts correct, all but two demonstrated an increase in at least half of the weeks. Two students did not demonstrate consistent growth in any of the weeks. The administered posttest was again analyzed for the range, mean, and median. The range of this data set went from five to sixty-seven. The average number of correct facts was thirty-nine. The median for this data set was forty-six, which is much closer to the mean than the pretest data set.
Conclusions
Describe your tentative conclusions from your data analysis.
• Daily single-digit multiplication fluency drills improve automaticity with math facts for the majority of students. • Some students do not achieve increased automaticity of single-digit multiplication facts with daily fluency drills.
Implications
Describe the importance of your findings for teaching and learning in our school.
If incorporated into our mathematics program, daily fluency drills have the potential to increase automaticity with single-digit multiplication facts. This was achieved with minimal expenditure of class time and no new resources purchased.
Describe future research you or others could do as a follow-up to this study.
• Why did a small number of students not achieve increased automaticity with this practice? • Will the increased automaticity with single-digit multiplication continue without this intervention?

TEACHER ACTION RESEARCH PROJECT

Staff Member's Name:	School Year:
I will be working to implement this plan: _____ Individually _____ In a Group. If in a group, please list group members:	
Problem Identification	
Interest Area:	
Literature Reviewed:	
Problem Statement:	
Research Question:	
Data Collection Methods	
Data Source 1 (What and How)	
Data Source 2 (What and How)	
Data Source 3 (What and How)	
Implementation Schedule	
Tasks	Time Line

TEACHER ACTION RESEARCH REPORT

Data Analysis
Provide a narrative summary of your collected and analyzed data. If appropriate, please attach graphs and tables to this summary.
Conclusions
Describe your tentative conclusions from your data analysis.
Implications
Describe the importance of your findings for teaching and learning in our school.
Describe future research you or others could do as a follow-up to this study.

· 6 ·

Examining Student Work

𝓑ringing teachers together to examine student work is a means for developing common criteria and common expectations. Focusing teacher dialogue on real artifacts can surface differences in teacher expectations and teaching practices. In turn, this increase in consistency can lead to improvements in instructional and assessment practices.

Examining student work is done for at least four reasons. First, a team of teachers may seek to create benchmarks for standards by agreeing on what varying levels of quality look like. Second, teachers may seek to understand if student learning is meeting specific standards. Third, teachers may seek to learn more about students' thinking and learning needs. Lastly, a teacher may seek advice for solving a dilemma or problem related to instruction.

When reviewing student work, it is essential that the focus remain on practices, not people. The goals are to understand student thinking and encourage self-reflection, not judge people. Thus, for this process to work, teachers must trust one another enough to be vulnerable to constructive criticism. If colleagues are unwilling to be honest, then the process will become one of going through the motions. Structured protocols can assist with creating an atmosphere conducive to exposing struggles and failures with colleagues.

Effective examination of student work requires the use of protocols. Structuring the method for analyzing student work is crucial if the goal is to achieve reflective dialogue. This chapter contains four protocols, one for each of the purposes identified here. A teacher leader can use these protocols with an individual teacher or with small groups who share a common need.

CREATING BENCHMARKS

Procedure:
1. Invite teachers to bring a work sample from three randomly selected students.
2. Using a common scoring rubric, each participant should individually review the student work product and assign scores.
3. Share and then compare ratings. Discuss any differences in ratings, encouraging an explanation for why the product was given the assigned score.
4. Attempt to reach consensus on the scores.
5. Use the consensus products as benchmarks for levels of quality of student work.

MEETING STANDARDS

Procedure:
1. Invite teachers to select a random sample of work completed by students.
2. Sort each student product into the appropriate category, and then record support for each decision. It is important to be specific, using criteria and indicators from a rubric or other district resource (see table 6.1).

Table 6.1

Below Standard	Meets Standard	Above Standard
What evidence shows that this work is below the standard?	What evidence shows that this work meets the standard?	What evidence shows that this work is above the standard?

3. After completing the entire set of student products, complete the following chart in table 6.2.

Table 6.2

Below Standard	Meets Standard	Above Standard
How many products fall in this category? % of group: _____	How many products fall in this category? % of group: _____	How many products fall in this category? % of group: _____

4. Discuss what has been learned by completing this exercise, and consider what, if any, next steps are required as a result.

STUDENT THINKING AND LEARNING NEEDS

Procedure:
1. Invite teachers to bring a set of completed and corrected papers to the meeting. These papers should have been scored using a common rubric.
2. Sort the papers into the categories of below standard, meeting standard, and above standard.
3. For the papers identified as below standard, examine the products to determine if there is a pattern of common errors students are making.
4. Discuss steps that can be taken to move students from the below-standard to the meeting-standard category.

INDIVIDUAL STUDENT LEARNING NEEDS

Procedure:
1. Invite teachers to bring four work products (from different assignments) created by a struggling student to the meeting.
2. Using a common rubric, take turns looking at each assignment. Attempt to determine which skills the student is not meeting for each assignment.
3. Examine the ratings to determine if there is a pattern or trend in the student's errors.
4. Describe the actions the teacher might take to improve the student's learning. Use the chart in table 6.3 to structure the process.

Table 6.3

Product type or topic	List several skills the student is not meeting.	What one skill could the student focus on to improve the quality of the product?	What could the teacher do to move the student to the next level of learning?
1.			
2.			
3.			
4.			

· 7 ·

Mentor Program Coordinator Materials

INTRODUCTION

If you are a teacher leader assigned the responsibility of managing and leading a teacher mentoring program, it can be overwhelming. Teacher mentoring programs are complex and crucial. Hopefully your school or district has supports in place to guide and assist you. Unfortunately, this is sometimes not the case. The materials in this chapter are meant to fill this void.

The first section of the chapter contains the materials needed to plan, coordinate, and evaluate a mentoring program. These materials are meant for the mentor program coordinator. The mentor handbook is meant for the mentors. It is a resource to assist mentors with fulfilling their responsibilities.

This chapter concludes with a series of monthly mentoring logs. It is highly recommended that the mentor program coordinator requires mentors to complete these logs and submit them for review. With all the distractions associated with the nature of a school year, it is easy to let mentoring activities get pushed aside. This is especially true after the logistical issues associated with the beginning of the year are complete.

The goal of a quality mentoring program is to provide support throughout the mentee's entire first year and possibly beyond. Mentoring logs are a form of accountability that encourages meeting this goal. As with all such tools, the materials in this chapter will need to be modified to fit local requirements.

72 *Chapter 7*

MENTORING PROGRAM COORDINATOR CHECKLIST

July

- Conduct mentor training.
- Facilitate mentor-mentee introductions.

August

- Match mentor-mentees for late hires. Provide additional mentor training sessions if necessary.

September

- Receive and review mentor logs.

October

- Receive and review mentor logs.

November

- Receive and review mentor logs.

December

- Receive and review mentor logs.
- Have a midyear mentor meeting to review progress, celebrate success, and address concerns or issues.

January

- Receive and review mentor logs.

February

- Receive and review mentor logs.

March

- Receive and review mentor logs.

April

- Receive and review mentor logs.
- Advertise for mentor teachers. Receive and review applications.

May

- Distribute, collect, and analyze mentor and mentee program surveys.
- Make recommendations for appropriate program revisions.

June

- Finalize pairing of mentors and mentees.
- Communicate pairing of mentors and mentees to all relevant parties.
- Finalize mentor training dates and materials.
- Have the end-of-year mentor-mentee celebration.

MENTOR TEACHER APPLICATION

Mentoring a novice teacher is both an awesome opportunity and a major responsibility. As a mentor, you are expected to serve as a role model, guide, caring colleague, resource, and coach. The words and actions of a mentor teacher make a significant impression on a novice teacher at a very impressionable point in their career. Therefore, to serve as a mentor, each teacher must complete a one-time application. The purpose of this application is to ensure the mentor meets the basic qualifications for serving as an effective mentor.

The mentor teacher must:

- be a certified teacher with a minimum of three years of experience in the school district.
- have at least two consecutive years of summative evaluation ratings that demonstrate proficiency with district teaching standards.
- agree to complete mentor training and be able to devote the time necessary for completing mentor responsibilities.
- be recognized by colleagues and administrators as demonstrating high levels of professional behavior.

Please complete all sections. If a section does not apply, indicate this by putting "N/A." Upon completion, please return to the mentoring coordinator.

Name of Applicant:	
Bachelor's Degree Major: Minor:	
Master's Degree Major:	
Certifications/Endorsements:	
Current Teaching Assignment: Grade Level: Number of Years in Current Assignment:	
Total Number of Years of Teaching Experience:	
Why do you want to serve as a mentor?	
What qualifies you to be a mentor?	
Teacher's Signature:	Date:
Direct Supervisor's Signature:	Date:

SAMPLE FOUR-HOUR MENTOR TRAINING AGENDA

Opening Activities (15 minutes)

Introduction to Mentoring (30 minutes)
- Definition
- Benefits
- Roles
- Characteristics of Effective Programs

Principles of Adult Learning (30 minutes)
- First-Year Teacher Development
- Mentor-Mentee Relationship Development

Communication Skills for Successful Mentoring (30 minutes)
- Trust
- Relationship Building
- Verbal and Nonverbal Communication Skills

Observation/Coaching Cycle (120 minutes)
- Planning Conference
- Observation
- Postconference
- Collaborative Analysis of Student Work
- Observation of Mentor's Classroom

Program Implementation Details (15 minutes)
- Mentor Log Completion
- Logistical Issues

Closing Activities (15 minutes)

LETTER IDENTIFYING MENTEE

Date:

Dear (insert staff member's name):

Congratulations! You have been selected to serve as a mentor during the (insert school year). Prior to serving as a mentor, it is required that you receive mentor training. The date for this training will be (insert date) from (insert times). The location for the training will be (insert location). You do not need to bring anything with you to this training. The agenda for this training is attached. Below is the contact information for your assigned mentee should you wish to reach out and introduce yourself:

- The name of the staff member you will mentoring is: (insert name)
- The e-mail address for this staff member is: (insert e-mail address)
- The phone number for this staff member is: (insert phone number)

I look forward to working with you to ensure the successful transition of our new staff to the school district.

Sincerely,
(your name)

Cc: Personnel File

LETTER IDENTIFYING MENTOR TEACHER

Date:

Dear (insert teacher name):

Welcome to the (insert name of school district) District. I want you to have a professionally rewarding and successful school year. (Insert mentor's name) has been assigned to serve as your mentor for the upcoming school year. Your mentor teacher will help you with school policies and procedures as well as curriculum requirements. In addition, your mentor will provide you with encouragement and support as you create educational opportunities for your students.

Again, welcome to the (insert name of school district) District. I am pleased to have you joining our staff.

Sincerely,
(your name)

MENTOR PROGRAM SURVEY

Mentor Version

Directions: We would like your perception of the district mentoring program. Results will be analyzed and used to improve the program for future participants. Please choose the appropriate response for each question, and then return it to the mentoring program coordinator. Do not write your name on this survey.

Question				
Mentor training prepared me to serve as a mentor.	Strongly Agree	Agree	Disagree	Strongly Disagree
Mentor responsibilities were clear.	Strongly Agree	Agree	Disagree	Strongly Disagree
I would agree to serve as a mentor again.	Strongly Agree	Agree	Disagree	Strongly Disagree
The mentor program coordinator was easily accessible and easy to speak with when necessary.	Strongly Agree	Agree	Disagree	Strongly Disagree
I had adequate time to meet with my mentee.	Strongly Agree	Agree	Disagree	Strongly Disagree
My relationship with my mentee was positive.	Strongly Agree	Agree	Disagree	Strongly Disagree
The help I provided my mentee was important and valuable.	Strongly Agree	Agree	Disagree	Strongly Disagree
Mentoring was a positive experience for me.	Strongly Agree	Agree	Disagree	Strongly Disagree
The most effective parts of the mentoring program were . . .				
The least effective parts of the mentoring program were . . .				
Suggestions I have for improving the mentoring program are . . .				

Mentee Version

Directions: We would like your perception of the district mentoring program. Results will be analyzed and used to improve the program for future participants. Please choose the appropriate response for each question and then return it to the mentoring program coordinator. Do not write your name on this survey.

Question				
My mentor was accessible and available.	Strongly Agree	Agree	Disagree	Strongly Disagree
My mentor communicated with me regularly.	Strongly Agree	Agree	Disagree	Strongly Disagree
My mentor demonstrated interest in my success.	Strongly Agree	Agree	Disagree	Strongly Disagree
I trust my mentor.	Strongly Agree	Agree	Disagree	Strongly Disagree
My mentor and I met often enough.	Strongly Agree	Agree	Disagree	Strongly Disagree
My mentor and I had a positive relationship.	Strongly Agree	Agree	Disagree	Strongly Disagree
My mentor provided me with valuable assistance.	Strongly Agree	Agree	Disagree	Strongly Disagree
The mentoring experience was positive for me.	Strongly Agree	Agree	Disagree	Strongly Disagree

The most effective parts of the mentoring program were . . .

The least effective parts of the mentoring program were . . .

Suggestions I have for improving the mentoring program are . . .

MENTOR COORDINATOR PROGRAM EVALUATION

1. Did the mentor program run as planned? Why or why not?
2. What were the strengths identified in the surveys?
3. What were the areas identified as needing improvement in the surveys?
4. Based on the information from the surveys, what aspects of the mentor program would you like to improve?
5. How could others in the district partner with you to further assist you in improving this program?

MENTOR HANDBOOK

Congratulations on being chosen to mentor a novice teacher. This selection is a testament to your high level of professionalism and your instructional expertise. Mentoring a novice teacher is both an awesome opportunity and a major responsibility. As a mentor, you are expected to fill the following roles:

- Role Model
- Guide
- Caring Colleague
- Resource
- Coach

Your words and actions will make a significant impression on the novice teacher you are mentoring. What you say and how you act will serve as the model that shapes their professional behavior. This will be especially true when you are handling difficult or sensitive situations. You were chosen for this role because the district believes you set the example that we seek for our staff members.

As their guide, you will be helping the novice teacher understand the multitude of procedures required for the operation of our school and district. Things that veteran teachers may take for granted are brand new to the novice teacher. Everything from making photocopies to scheduling parent-teacher conferences will need some degree of explanation. Furthermore, you will be essential for helping the novice teacher navigate the social relationships that exist within your building.

At the core of mentoring is the relationship between the mentor and the new teacher. Trust is the determining factor that will make this relationship either flourish or perish. A new teacher needs to trust a mentor enough to share both their successes and their mistakes without judgment. Your mentee needs to be assured that you will keep all communications between the two of you private. Even speaking of the mentee in a complimentary way shouldn't be done without first asking their permission. Trust can be difficult to establish, but it can be easily destroyed.

Furthermore, the novice must understand that you are not there to evaluate or judge them. Instead, they must believe that you are there to help them—and only help them. Additionally, they need to understand that you will do everything within reason to help them succeed.

As a mentor, you will serve as an invaluable instructional resource. Novice teachers do not have years of instructional plans, materials, and resources to draw from. In fact, they often do not yet know what will and will not work in their classroom. You can provide them with model plans to follow and share your classroom materials and resources. Furthermore, you can direct them to where they can find additional resources, both within and outside the school. Even better, if possible, you can collaborate with the novice teacher to develop plans. They will benefit greatly from learning how a professional teacher prepares for instruction.

The final role you will assume is that of an instructional coach. Reviewing the content of Matthew J. Jennings's book *From First Year to First Rate* (Lanham, MD: Rowman and Littlefield, 2021) with them will help the novice teacher deepen their understanding of the crucial components of effective teaching. In addition, inviting them to observe your use of any of these strategies will provide the novice teacher with a real-life example of effective implementation. Lastly, observing their use of these strategies will provide you with the opportunity to offer feedback the novice teacher can use for growth.

Mentoring Skills

Knowing how to teach and teaching someone else how to teach are two very different skills. This section is intended to provide you with the basic skills you require to mentor effectively. The first and perhaps most important skills required are interpersonal. An interpersonal skill that will build trust and encourage the mentee to express him- or herself freely is active listening.

Active listening is hard work because we usually only listen long enough to hear what we need to make our next point of agreement or disagreement. Follow these recommendations to improve your active listening skills:

- Refrain from interrupting the person speaking; don't be afraid of silence.
- If there is not enough time to listen actively, then say so.

- Paraphrase. Listen to what is being said without distraction, then summarize what you have heard and understood (e.g., "I think I hear you saying that you are frustrated by the amount of time it takes students to line up for recess.").
- Check with the speaker to make sure that your interpretation of what you have heard is correct (e.g., "It sounds like you don't think your students are motivated to complete their homework. Is that correct?").
- Probe to expand on ideas, unearth assumptions, and explore applications (e.g., "Help me understand what led you to that conclusion.").
- Be aware of your nonverbal behaviors. Making eye contact communicates interest and helps you establish rapport. Smiling indicates warmth and openness in communication. Good posture conveys poise and confidence.

Another skill that is required to be an effective mentor is providing quality feedback. It stands to reason that if a teacher does not know what he or she is doing right or wrong, then it will be difficult for them to improve their knowledge or skill. To improve the quality of feedback you provide, practice the following behaviors:

- Be honest and genuine, but say what you mean without being mean. Tact is important.
- Avoid overwhelming the mentee. It is better to offer advice in small doses and work on one area for improvement at a time. One small success at a time will lead to bigger victories as the teacher's skill level and knowledge increases.
- Be descriptive (e.g., "When you were presenting instruction, three of the students were viewing their phones.") instead of evaluative (e.g., "Your instructional presentation skills were boring.").
- Be future oriented. Specify the strategies a teacher is performing correctly and effectively as well as which strategies require changes moving forward because they were demonstrated with errors or omissions. You can also provide feedback on strategies a teacher could have used in the lesson but didn't. This will give them ideas for future lessons.

Conducting Classroom Visitations with Your Mentee

One situation in which you will have to provide feedback is the observation of your mentee's teaching. The process for observation will be guided by the protocols provided here. The mentee will complete the preobservation conference protocol form. You will then meet to discuss the contents of this form and establish how data will be collected. During your observation, you will collect student and teacher evidence related to the focus of the observation. Shortly after the observation, you will make notes and list ideas or questions for discussion. Lastly, you will meet and discuss the observation using the postconference protocol procedure.

COACHING FORMS PREOBSERVATION CONFERENCE PROTOCOL

This section is to be completed by the mentee before the preobservation meeting:

- What is the objective for this lesson?
- What specifically do you want me to look for?
- Is there anything specific you want me to know about this class or lesson prior to the observation?
- When will the observation be, and how long will it take place?
- When and where will we meet after the observation to reflect on the lesson?

COACHING OBSERVATION FORM

Teacher Name:
Observer Name:
Date:
Time:
Instructional Focus:

Teacher Evidence	Student Evidence
Observation Notes	**Ideas and Questions**

POSTOBSERVATION CONFERENCE PROTOCOL

- Mentee describes how he or she thinks the lesson went.
- Based on the focus area for the observation, discuss what the mentor observed.
- Collaborative reflection on the observations: What does the gathered data mean?
- Collaborative discussion of observation results for future practice: What can the mentee do differently to improve, and how can he or she do it?

Collaborative Analysis of Student Work

In addition to observing your mentee's instruction, there are at least two other activities you will complete together. One of these activities is collaborative analysis of student work. Four times throughout the year, you and your mentee will be expected to collaboratively examine student work. The purpose for this activity is to assist the mentee with developing effective assessment skills. The process to be used is as follows:

1. Request that your mentee select samples of student work that appear to meet the following criteria:
   - Select one student product that **demonstrates achievement** of the instructional goal.
   - Select one student product that **may demonstrate** achievement of the instructional goal.
   - Select one student product that **does not demonstrate** achievement of the instructional goal.
2. Separately analyze the student product to determine appropriate ratings with the district- or teacher-created rubric.
3. Compare ratings, discussing similarities and differences.
4. Select one of the student products, and jointly analyze it further for the following:
   - What feedback can be provided to this student?
   - What should be the next step in the learning progression for this student?
5. Repeat for the other two student products if time permits.

Mentee Observing Mentor's Classroom

Novice teachers benefit greatly from seeing effective instructional strategies in action. As a mentor, having your mentee observe you (or another master teacher) will help them develop a vision of effective instruction. You will complete this activity a minimum of two times during the year.

To be most effective, the lesson should be connected to an area of the mentee's interest or need. Thus, prior to the lesson, share your lesson plan and collaboratively establish the purpose for the observation. Be clear about what the mentee will focus on during the observed lesson.

In addition, the mentee must be actively engaged during the lesson. The mentee should take notes during the observation. This can be structured via a checklist of teacher and student "look for's," or it can be unstructured. In either case, the mentee's observation notes can serve as a springboard for discussion in a follow-up conference.

Try to have the postobservation conference as soon as possible. The same day is best for processing of the activity. In the postobservation conference, encourage the mentee to ask questions about what you did and why. In addition, discuss how the observed activities could be translated to their own classroom.

Supporting the Formal Induction Program

As a mentor, there are activities from the induction program that you can assist your mentee in completing:

- Your mentee is required to create and submit a portfolio. You can assist them with selecting and reflecting on their documents and then review the portfolio with them prior to submission.
- Your mentee is required to record and reflect on video of their teaching. With their permission, you can watch the recording with them and assist them with the required reflection.
- Your mentee is required to collect and analyze student survey data. You can review and discuss this data with them.
- Your mentee will be participating in a study group based on the content of *From First Year to First Rate*. Review the contents of the reading with your mentee. In addition, follow up with them after their study group meetings to determine if they have any further questions or concerns.

Mentor Logs

A structured calendar of guiding questions and suggested tasks provides organization to the mentoring process. The following monthly mentoring guides provide a template for much of what must be accomplished by a new teacher during their first year. These guides are not all-inclusive, as some tasks may differ depending on the requirements of individual schools or departments. Appropriate adjustments of tasks should be made when necessary and appropriate.

The meeting dates/times and brief descriptions of activities are an accountability mechanism that serve as documentation of meeting mentoring expectations. This section, plus the reflection prompts for the mentor, must be completed monthly. Mentoring must be thought of as an ongoing, deepening, year-long relationship focused on improving student learning. The following guides will serve to meet this purpose.

July Mentoring Guide	
Typical Teacher Phase: Anticipation	**Mentoring Priorities:** Mentee Preparation
Meeting Dates/Times	**Brief Description of Activities**
Logistics	**Possible Discussion Questions**
• Establish two meeting dates for August, one in the early part of the month that will last for one to two hours and a second in the middle of the month that will last at least a half-day.	• What do you already know about this community and school? • What is your experience in organizing a classroom? • What do you need from me? • About what do you feel most concerned?
Informational Tasks	**Instructional Tasks**
• Make sure your mentee has a copy of the staff directory. If possible, introduce him or her to the custodians, secretaries, and other available teachers. • Share information with the mentee on the history and cultural makeup of the town. • Make sure the mentee has a copy of staff and student handbooks. Provide clarification on any confusing items. • Provide your mentee with a tour of the facility.	• Make sure your mentee has access to or copies of the necessary curriculum materials. • If available, make sure your mentee has a copy of their class list and their assigned schedule.
Management Tasks	**Personal Tasks**
• Assist the mentee with acquiring the classroom resources and materials needed to start the year. Requisition any essential supplies. • Ensure your mentee has a copy of the school calendar.	• Introduce yourself and spend some time getting to know the personal and professional background of your mentee.
Reflections	
• This month, as I prepared my mentee for the beginning of the school year, the following things stood out to me . . . • Something I will do differently next time is . . .	

August Mentoring Guide	
Typical Teacher Phase: Anticipation	**Mentoring Priorities:** Mentee Preparation
Meeting Dates/Times	**Brief Description of Activities**
Logistics	**Possible Discussion Questions**
• Establish a weekly meeting date and time for the first month of the school year. In addition, discuss the process that will be used to check in daily during the first week of school.	• What questions do the resources provided to you pose? • How can I support you right now?
Informational Tasks	**Instructional Tasks**
• Review district and school policies and procedures related to the following: —Student conduct —Reporting abuse and neglect —School closings —Emergency drills and procedures —Sending students to the nurse —Making copies —Teacher arrival and dismissal —Instructional planning —Grading	• Collaboratively develop or at a minimum review and make suggestions on your mentee's first-day-of-school plans. • Review report card format. • Make sure your mentee has created a set of emergency substitute plans. Review these plans and suggest any necessary revisions.
Management Tasks	**Interpersonal Tasks**
• Collaboratively set up your mentee's classroom or at a minimum review and make suggestions for how your mentee sets up their room. • Make sure your mentee has sufficient copies of all necessary forms.	• Assess your mentee with introducing him- or herself to student and parents prior to the start of the school year.
Reflections	
• This month, as I prepared my mentee for the beginning of the school year, the following things stood out for me . . . • Something I will do differently next time is . . .	

September Mentoring Guide	
Typical Teacher Phase: Survival	**Mentoring Priorities:** Interact often, including socially; listen and engage in joint problem solving; assist with task completion.
Meeting Dates/Times	**Brief Description of Activities**
Logistics	**Possible Discussion Questions**
• Establish a weekly meeting time for the month of October. • Plan for your mentee to observe your classroom at least once.	• What is going well? • What is the biggest issue you are facing? • What problems have you encountered? • How are you taking care of yourself?
Informational Tasks	**Instructional Tasks**
• Review the district teacher evaluation process and documents with your mentee. • Assist your mentee with preparing for open house. • Explain procedures for accessing student records. • Explain procedures for calling in sick and getting a substitute teacher. • Review field trip procedures. • Review student attendance procedures.	• Cocreate or review and provide feedback on initial units of instruction. • Review student IEPs and ESL needs. Discuss implications of identified requirements and needs for your mentee. • If a paraprofessional is assigned to the classroom, discuss how to use their assistance most effectively. • If appropriate, collaboratively assess samples of student work.
Management Tasks	**Interpersonal Tasks**
• Discuss with your mentee the importance of reinforcing and being consistent with expectations, rules, and routines. • Review expectations for any assigned duty periods. • Make sure your mentee is correcting, recording, and returning student work in a timely manner.	• Complete introductions of your mentee to all appropriate staff. • Discuss strategies for building positive and appropriate student relationships. • Discuss strategies for maintaining appropriate, proactive, and positive parent communication.
Reflections	
• Something I would like to work on together with my mentee is . . . • Something I learned from my mentee is . . .	

October Mentoring Guide	
Typical Teacher Phase: Survival	**Mentoring Priorities:** Interact often, including socially; listen and engage in joint problem solving; assist with task completion.
Meeting Dates/Times	**Brief Description of Activities**
Logistics	**Possible Discussion Questions**
• Establish a weekly meeting time for November. • Schedule a peer observation of your mentee's classroom.	• What is going well in your classroom? • What would you like to focus on for improvement? • What can I do to assist you? • What are you doing to take care of yourself?
Informational Tasks	**Instructional Tasks**
• Review procedures for student progress reports. • Review policies on holiday celebrations. • Discuss the importance of confidentiality.	• Have your mentee observe your classroom and focus on the most appropriate aspects for their needs. Debrief after the observation. • Review and discuss instructional plans.
Management Tasks	**Interpersonal Tasks**
• Discuss any issues or concerns related to behavior management. • Discuss ideas for time management.	• Encourage continued parental communication. • Discuss strategies for managing stress.
Reflections	
• What I am learning about being a mentor is . . . • I know that my mentoring is helpful because . . .	

November Mentoring Guide	
Typical Teacher Phase: Disillusionment	**Mentoring Priorities:** Listening, providing support and encouragement, and setting short-term goals.
Meeting Dates/Times	**Brief Description of Activities**
Logistics	**Possible Discussion Questions**
• Establish a weekly meeting time for December.	• What is going well in your classroom? • What would you like to focus on for improvement? • What can I do to assist you? • What are you doing to take care of yourself?
Informational Tasks	**Instructional Tasks**
• Review procedures for referring a student to the student support team. • Make sure the mentee is aware of any school staff gatherings. Encourage attendance. • Review content of standardized state and district testing requirements.	• Conduct a peer observation of your mentee. Provide feedback from the observation. • Review the methods the mentee is using to keep students informed of their academic progress.
Management Tasks	**Interpersonal Tasks**
• Discuss any continuing issues or concerns related to behavior management.	• Help your mentee prepare for parent-teacher conferences. • Discuss strategies for managing stress.
Reflections	
• How are you using your strengths and interests in your role as a mentor? • What will you do differently next month?	

December Mentoring Guide	
Typical Teacher Phase: Disillusionment	**Mentoring Priorities:** Listening, providing support and encouragement, and setting short-term goals.
Meeting Dates/Times	**Brief Description of Activities**
Logistics	**Possible Discussion Questions**
• Review the meeting schedule. Is the current frequency of meetings still appropriate, or should revisions be made starting in January? Set the agreed-upon times for meeting after break.	• What is going well in your classroom? • What would you like to focus on for improvement? • What can I do to assist you? • What are you doing to take care of yourself? • What, if anything, might you want to change after the school break?
Informational Tasks	**Instructional Tasks**
• N/A	• If appropriate, collaboratively assess student work samples. • Review the results of any midyear assessment data, and discuss implications.
Management Tasks	**Interpersonal Tasks**
• Discuss any continuing issues or concerns related to behavior management.	• Encourage your mentee to participate in any staff holiday activities. • Discuss strategies for managing stress. • Congratulate your mentee on making it to this point in the year. Emphasize the positives they have accomplished.
Reflections	
• To be a better mentor I will . . . • The most important things I have learned during the first half of the year are . . .	

January Mentoring Guide	
Typical Teacher Phase: Rejuvenation	**Mentoring Priorities:** Reflection, networking, and professional growth.
Meeting Dates/Times	**Brief Description of Activities**
Logistics	**Possible Discussion Questions**
• Set agreed-upon times for meeting in February. • Arrange a date and time for your mentee to observe in your classroom.	• What is going well in your classroom? • What would you like to focus on for improvement? • What can I do to assist you? • What are you doing to take care of yourself?
Informational Tasks	**Instructional Tasks**
• Review district policies related to professionalism and confidentiality. • Review any previously created statements of teaching philosophy. Discuss changes to ideals and beliefs about teaching.	• Set instructional and personal goals for the second half of the year. • Discuss professional development opportunities outside the school district and how to apply for attendance. • If appropriate, collaboratively assess student work samples.
Management Tasks	**Interpersonal Tasks**
• Discuss any continuing issues or concerns related to behavior management. • Discuss the importance of reviewing rules, procedures, and routines after break.	• Encourage continued parental communication.
Reflections	
• What I like most about being a mentor is . . . • As a mentor, I find it frustrating that . . .	

February Mentoring Guide	
Typical Teacher Phase: Rejuvenation	**Mentoring Priorities:** Reflection, networking, and professional growth.
Meeting Dates/Times	**Brief Description of Activities**
Logistics	**Possible Discussion Questions**
• Set the agreed-upon times for meeting in March. • Arrange a date and time for you to conduct a peer observation in your mentee's classroom.	• What is going well in your classroom? • What would you like to focus on for improvement? • What can I do to assist you? • How are you doing in reaching the agreed-upon instructional and personal goals? • Are you setting time aside for exercise, relaxation, family, and friends?
Informational Tasks	**Instructional Tasks**
• Review district homework policies. Discuss ways to use homework appropriately. • Review district policies on student promotion to the next grade level. • Review procedures for developing a classroom budget.	• Have your mentee observe your classroom. Debrief the visit. • Review the requirements for upcoming state or district testing, and provide suggestions for preparing students to perform at their best. • If appropriate, collaboratively assess student work samples.
Management Tasks	**Interpersonal Tasks**
• Discuss any continuing issues or concerns related to behavior management.	• Encourage continued parental communication.
Reflections	
• It is difficult to . . . • My mentee needs to improve at . . .	

March Mentoring Guide	
Typical Teacher Phase: Rejuvenation	**Mentoring Priorities:** Reflection, networking, and professional growth.
Meeting Dates/Times	**Brief Description of Activities**
Logistics	**Possible Discussion Questions**
• Set the agreed-upon times for meeting in April.	• What is going well in your classroom? • What would you like to focus on for improvement? • What can I do to assist you? • Have you connected with fellow novice teachers? • Do you have any questions or concerns about school politics?
Informational Tasks	**Instructional Tasks**
• Review student dress code. • Review opportunities for staff involvement in school improvement. Encourage appropriate involvement for the subsequent school year.	• Observe your mentee. Conference with your mentee afterward to discuss observation. • Help your mentee prepare for any parent-teacher conferences.
Management Tasks	**Interpersonal Tasks**
• Discuss any continuing issues or concerns related to behavior management.	• Encourage continued parental communication.
Reflections	
• I am pleased . . . • Mentoring is like . . . • Serving as a mentor is helping me . . .	

Chapter 7

April Mentoring Guide	
Typical Teacher Phase: Rejuvenation	**Mentoring Priorities:** Reflection, networking, and professional growth.
Meeting Dates/Times	**Brief Description of Activities**
Logistics	**Possible Discussion Questions**
• Set the agreed-upon times for meeting in May.	• What is going well in your classroom? • What would you like to focus on for improvement? • What can I do to assist you? • What are your questions about the process of being rehired? • What is the status of your progress toward your goals for the second half of the school year?
Informational Tasks	**Instructional Tasks**
• Review school and district policies regarding end-of-year activities, assemblies, and parties. • Review the district teacher evaluation standards.	• Review unit plans. • If appropriate, collaboratively assess samples of student work.
Management Tasks	**Interpersonal Tasks**
• Discuss any continuing issues or concerns related to behavior management.	• Prepare your mentee for their end-of-year summative conference with their supervisor.
Reflections	
• I am surprised by . . . • How have my mentoring skills developed? • What more do I need to learn to continue improving as a mentor?	

May Mentoring Guide	
Typical Teacher Phase: Reflection	**Mentoring Priorities:** Reflection, planning.
Meeting Dates/Times	**Brief Description of Activities**
Logistics	**Possible Discussion Questions**
• Set an agreed-upon time for celebrating the conclusion of the year.	• What is going well in your classroom? • What would you like to focus on for improvement? • What can I do to assist you? • What ideas do you have that you want to incorporate into the next school year?
Informational Tasks	**Instructional Tasks**
• Review procedures for end-of-school-year tasks.	• Plan for participation in relevant summer professional development activities.
Management Tasks	**Interpersonal Tasks**
• Encourage your mentee to express interest in any appropriate school improvement opportunities for the subsequent school year.	• Discuss the importance of finishing the school year strong and continuing to build relationships with parents, staff, and students.
Reflections	
• An area of growth I observed in my mentee is . . . • What I have learned about mentoring is . . .	

June Mentoring Guide

June Mentoring Guide	
Typical Teacher Phase: Reflection	**Mentoring Priorities:** Reflection, planning.
Meeting Dates/Times	**Brief Description of Activities**
Logistics	**Possible Discussion Questions**
• N/A	• What did you learn about yourself as a teacher this year? • What did you learn about your students and their families this year? • How can I help you complete the year and the required school-closing tasks?
Informational Tasks	**Instructional Tasks**
• Review procedures for end-of-school-year tasks.	• Discuss the importance of continuing to work on academics through to the end of the school year.
Management Tasks	**Interpersonal Tasks**
• Help your mentee complete all required paperwork for the end of the school year. • Assist your mentee with the tasks required for closing the classroom. • Review unique classroom management needs and concerns related to the end of the school year.	• Help your mentee craft a final communication to parents. • Make sure your mentee has plans to finish the school year with students on a positive note.
Reflections	
• This year as a mentor, I have learned . . . • One thing I would change about the mentoring program is . . . • I benefited most from . . .	

About the Author

Dr. **Matthew J. Jennings** is a twenty-eight-year veteran of public education. He has served as a classroom teacher, supervisor of instruction, director of special services, director of human resources, principal, assistant superintendent, and superintendent. He is the author of fourteen books and eleven journal articles. He has presented at numerous state, regional, and national conferences. In addition to his work as a public educator, he has also served as an adjunct professor for Rutgers University and the College of New Jersey. He can be reached at mattmarz1994@gmail.com.

www.ingramcontent.com/pod-product-compliance
Lightning Source LLC
Chambersburg PA
CBHW030147240426
43672CB00005B/305